"Kendall Hoeft's depiction of childlike faith, joy, and wonder is a breath of fresh air. May you be fired up to approach God with the same childlike tenacity Hoeft writes about, and receive back the same freedom as you read!"

—TEHILLAH HARTMANN,
founder, Being Salt Co.

I0139640

"If you have never permitted yourself to freely express your praise to God, *Big God, Big Glory* might be the biggest little book you have ever read."

—RAY HUGHES,
author of *Sound of Heaven, Symphony of Earth*

"In her book *Big God, Big Glory*, Kendall Hoeft shares her passion for worshipping God authentically and artistically, and she calls us to join her. The book pushes us to examine boundaries in praise expression and to study the Bible to know whether they should exist as we in the North American church are accustomed. Using this springboard for thought, we can dig into a fuller understanding of how our 'Big God' does indeed require 'Big Glory.'"

—KARYN SMITH,
educator

"Creatives see things that others don't. And sometimes they see more clearly. *Big God, Big Glory* separates the wheat from the chaff and shines a light on the good in Christianity and following faith, all while giving grace and still gently shoving aside the kelp on the oar of the church. Every believer should read this, not just the artists."

—AUSTIN BIEL,
artist coach/producer

"Kendall Hoeft examines the often overlooked and undiscovered attributes of God like weirdness, art, play, and shine. She sprinkles in anecdotal stories amidst scriptural study to reveal how essential creativity, authenticity, and glory are to each of our faith-walks and worship-journeys. You can feel the purpose and the passion in each word and exploration of God's nature as the book blesses and challenges us to step into a more glorious calling."

—KATHLEEN MCGUIRE,
poet

"God has filled our believing hearts with His indescribable presence, pure love, and diverse gifts of the Spirit. I pray for the body of Christ to move beyond a somber worship performance and instead boldly rise up in praise and adoration to enjoy and glorify our Creator with everything He has placed within us. *Big God, Big Glory* is a breath of fresh air as it speaks the truth in love."

—MARY L. HALEY,
pastor, Connect2Christ Church

"Like a butterfly struggling to emerge, *Big God, Big Glory* is Kendall Hoeft's honest and raw-penned journey to express her freedom as she longs to soar in the glory of the presence of God."

—YVONNE DIEZ PETERS,
author of *Beyond the Dance*

"Kendall Hoeft gives a transparent, heartfelt account of her journey to find space to worship and glorify God with all her might as a creative artist. Her desire to be a Holy Spirit-inspired, Bible-based extravagant worshipper provides a challenging read! Hoeft moves us to partner with a creative God and to think on how to encourage creatives to reach and influence our culture with his light."

—MARY HAUCK,
co-founder and co-director, School of Worship Arts Training

"If you have a passion for worship or are intrigued by the concept of expressive worship within the church, then this book is for you. In a culture that often stifles both mourning and celebration, this book provides biblical permission and validation to boldly step out in faith, in our worship and beyond, to bring our big God big glory. After all, we will be worshipping Him forever."

—NANETTE BOYER,
director, Nanette Boyer Ballet Studio

# Big God, Big Glory

# Big God, Big Glory

*An Exploration of God's Creativity and*
*How We Were Created to Display His Glory*

KENDALL HOEFT

RESOURCE *Publications* · Eugene, Oregon

BIG GOD, BIG GLORY
An Exploration of God's Creativity and How We Were Created to Display
His Glory

Resource Publications
An Imprint of Wipf and Stock Publishers
199 W. 8th Ave., Suite 3
Eugene, OR 97401

www.wipfandstock.com

PAPERBACK ISBN: 979-8-3852-0335-2
HARDCOVER ISBN: 979-8-3852-0336-9
EBOOK ISBN: 979-8-3852-0337-6

04/23/24

That your joy may be full

JOHN 15

# Contents

# PART III   UPWARD AND ONWARD

DEAR READER,

Our God is big and glorious. In this book, we will examine some of God's attributes: aspects that should be responded to in who we are in Him. We, too, are brave, free, creative, weird, authentic, shiny, powerful, light, and holy. The purpose behind *Big God, Big Glory* is threefold.

Firstly, it was written for God. I believe He wanted me to write this book. He wants this message to be spoken, like light, into the universe. The title, *Big God, Big Glory*, followed me around. It followed me into the kitchen when I was boiling water for tea. It followed me into conversations and Facebook posts. It even followed me into bed at night. It followed me until, I could no longer resist bringing it into existence, "Okay Lord," I said, "I'll write the book."

*Big God, Big Glory* was birthed with an unquenchable desire for God to receive the glory that He is so worthy of. As we learn to walk in the fullness of our God-crafted expression, we declare His glory and shine for Him more brightly. As we, His living art, pull back the tarps that cover our true, authentic light, we reveal Christ to our church community and the world.

It is not our job to judge the artwork or hide it in the name of "humility." It is our job to put on one heck of an art show. We must have the platform at a height where the people can see His glorious, living art. We must be well-lit, so that His creativity and beautiful artistry can be displayed and seen.

> *Let your light shine before others,*
> *so that they may see your good (creative) works*
> *and give glory to your Father who is in Heaven.*
> (Matt 5:16)

Secondly, this book was written for you. *Big God, Big Glory* has come to life to give you more freedom and peace about who you are through an understanding of who God is. When we learn that God is joyful, gentle, and wild instead of harsh, distant, and solemn, we learn who we truly are and how to reflect Him in our lives and praise expression.

This book is for you, that your "joy may be complete" and that you might find true satisfaction through living out your God-given, glory-carrying purpose (John 15:11 NIV). I want you to be free, not suppressed—fulfilled and wholly alive.

Thirdly, this book was written for others. As you shine wildly and carry the glory of God, you will impact and encourage the souls around you. As you beam out authenticity, creativity, purity, and joy, others will see Jesus in a fresh, true way. You will carry stunning and lovely revelations of God the modern church is largely unaware of. As you walk strongly in freedom and unrelenting joy, you will be a living, dancing, breathing message that God is light: uncontainable and great.

As we seek to shine for His glory, we become clear and open channels, vessels of Him. *Big God, Big Glory* is a manual for glory-filled living. It is my prayer that it be used as an element of light in your lives, hearts, minds, and bodies. This book is a study of who God is and how we are created to display His glory.

To God be the glory,
Kendall

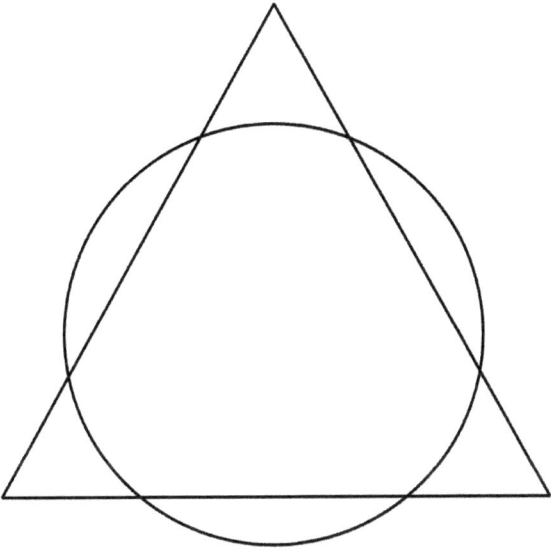

# PART I

## Big God, Big Glory

# I. BRAVE

## FAITH

Dear friend, you are brave. In picking up a wild book like this, you demonstrate faith and childlike curiosity. I believe you will be rewarded richly through it. Thank you for coming on this journey with me.

Bravery requires faith. You must believe in something to care enough to take a stand. Faith isn't just some hazy spiritual word. It involves risk, action, trust, and bravery. Faith is a jumping into the unknown based on a deep trust in, and love for, God. In the famous faith chapter, Hebrews 11, we see many examples of what it means to live a life of faith.

Noah, who built a ship in the middle of dry land, believed in something he couldn't see over what seemed to be real in the present, physical world. That is faith. We, too, are called to possibly appear "crazy" as we do heavenly things that are unusual in our current setting. Noah risked his reputation, for the greater glory of God. He cared more about his Father on the throne than others' opinions on the temporary earth around him. Noah's bravery communicated to God that he would choose Him over everything else. Because of Noah's faith and obedience, he became intimate with God (v. 7).

Abraham, another faith-filled man, saw something off in the distance. He believed in the visions God placed in his mind of a heavenly city. Abraham lived for heaven. He was more concerned with what existed in the mind of God and the eternal realities than about what was considered normal or what might be thought about him. He stepped out in brave faith. Trusting in God alone, he left his family and home, to journey to a new land that God promised to him.

Moses' parents saved their beautiful baby when the law sought to kill him. They choose faith and bravery, to protect their precious child. The law will always seek to control and stomp out life. The law brings death. God brings life abundantly. The law of God is love. Anything else is stifling the light.

Many of our contemporary, North American churches have laws. These laws give permission to worship in three ways: (1) raising one or two hands, (2) singing, and (3) clapping. Many churches are even more limited in the types of responses they allow. Some welcome only singing.

But praise and worship are more than singing, and more still than a confined list of acceptable-to-man expressions. Praise is the overflow of the soul. It is the fullness of all that a person carries: unpredictable and freshly authentic to each individual. Praise is the outpouring of our insides, as we bring our whole being (mind, spirit, and body) before the Lord. Praise is the children of God's authentic response to their great Father; and children, if encouraged, get very excited! These honest expressions of adoration, from God's kids of all ages, bring glory to God and are pleasing to Him.

Limiting our responses to God's goodness, greatness, and glory is not what God intended for His church. We cannot permit our understanding of what praise is, and what God desires in worship, to be formed merely by the history of the church's traditions and what is currently practiced. We must go deeper. I encourage you to question what you have experienced or think you know. Seek the Scriptures and humbly pray, so that God might receive all glory, honor, and praise, forever and ever. Amen.

# I. BRAVE

## VISION

Faith creates vision. What we don't see creates what we see. The spiritual vision, in each of our souls, is meant to manifest into the world. With a faith perspective, we live by what we believe based on the Bible and listening to God, not by what we see around us. In the realm of praise expression, this foundational aspect of faith is important. Taking our cues from the Holy Spirit in responding to God requires great faith.

Praising our Lord, in faith, often requires a stepping out. We must take the risk of being misunderstood, judged, and not accepted. Some will not understand why we jump for joy or run in freedom or dance in loving passion. Remember my friends that our praise is, firstly, for our Father in heaven. We must trust His leading and respond in liberty, knowing that He is well pleased. Let us lean on Jesus, the author and finisher of our faith. Let us rest on the approval and acceptance of God, as we dance, shout, jump, run, twirl, bow, and bend in faith.

# II. FREE

## *CHILDLIKENESS*

I'm going to be referring to children often in this book. That is because there is much to learn from their creativity, unabashed expression, innocence, and faith. Childlikeness is our true identity. It is who we are in our purest, uninhibited form. The qualities of spontaneity, joy, and purity are aspects of who God is and who we are created to be.

Children are close to the heart of God. As we live in the world, we must guard against being influenced in limiting ways. We must protect our relationship with God, so that we can live with integrity and freedom. When we read the lyrics we are singing at church, do we allow ourselves to shout out in excitement or spontaneously twirl around in excitement as children do? Do we allow our bodies to respond to God's goodness and express our joy? In what ways have we been unconsciously sculpted by the ways of the world and modified by societal norms? Are we slaves to the fear of what others might think or servants of the Most High?

Imagine a little boy at a jazz concert. His body is easily moved by the rhythm. Whether he is at the park, or church service or birthday party, he doesn't hesitate or restrain himself. He doesn't overthink the situation or censor himself based on what others might think of him. He simply moves to the music and enjoys it.

This is who we were created to be. The Bible talks about the quality of childlikeness and its importance. In the book of Matthew, Jesus says, "Unless you change and become like little children, you will never enter the kingdom of heaven" (18:3 NIV).

## II. FREE

I want to become more like an innocent little child in my ability to be in the moment, flowing in Him.

## RELEASING THE BODY

We are holistic creatures: mind, spirit, and body. Our praise expression is meant to flow out of the union and connectedness of our yoked being. You were created to praise Him and respond to Him "with all your heart and with all your soul and with all your strength and with all your mind" (Luke 10:27). This word "strength" refers to physical might. We are created to love the Lord with our bodies. What does it look like to respond to God with our bodies in praise?

Words translated as "praise," "rejoice," "worship," etc. in our English translations come from richer Hebrew words and meanings. Most of these praise words, in the original language, include a physical component. In other words, our bodies are meant to participate in praising God. In many of our modern North American churches, our minds are engaged and/or our hearts are engaged, but we have left the body behind. Our bodies are important to God. He wants all of us.

Romans 12:1 appeals to God's followers "to present your bodies as a living sacrifice, holy and acceptable to God, which is your spiritual worship." We are called to bring our bodies to Him in praise and worship, whether we feel like doing so or not. It could be argued that the more uncomfortable in the flesh someone is in moving their body, or dancing before the Lord, the larger and more poignant a sacrifice of praise they are offering up to God. Sacrifice is meant to be a surrender, a giving up, an offering of ourselves to God. It's meant to be costly. We're meant to feel it. This area of praise and worship provides an ideal opportunity to practice submitting ourselves to the Holy Spirit.

God Himself came into a body. "The Word became flesh and dwelt among us, and we beheld His glory" (John 1:14 NKJV). We now are stand-ins for Christ on this earth. We are vessels through which others can behold the glory of God. We, the church, are called "the body of Christ" (1 Cor 12:27).

# III. CREATIVE

## OUR CREATIVE GOD

The Bible begins with creativity. "In the beginning, God created" (Gen 1:1a). He created all that lives, moves, and has its being; the heavens, cosmos, everything. When we look at His creative works, we see the wildness and diversity of the artist. He could have made a boring, black and white world—a straight, functional reality, but He cares about design and color. God has a playful spirit. He is an artist and creative expressionist.

Often, in conversations about creativity in praise expression, someone will bring up "order in worship." Order in the church service is usually brought up as a way of proving that freedom in our worship should not exist, driven by the misconception that such imaginative expression is "out of order." There is to be an order to our worship, but it is God's order. We must be careful to base our ideas about "order" in our services on His design, not on man-based ideas of what we assume order is.

When we look at the rainforest, we don't find trees exactly the same, groomed into exact triangles to man's standards. Instead, we see God's unexpected order—through exuberance, diversity, mystery, divine complexity, and rugged beauty. Through this natural example, God demonstrates how wildness and perfect order are yoked together in Him. God Himself makes it clear that His divine order isn't what some expect it to be. God's order doesn't look like what man might assume it would. God's order might even look like chaos, to a non-spiritual eye.

It is vital that we seek to know God for who He actually is, not for who we presume He is, or who we think He "should" be. We must not make church services into our image; based on our ideas of what order ought to look like. Man must be careful not to run a church by his own order. Yes, there is to be a decency and order to a church service, but we must remember that this is God's order not ours.

Let us listen to God's heart and look at His artwork to know Him better. First Corinthians 2:14 says, "The natural person does not accept the things of the Spirit of God, for they are folly to him, and he is not able to understand them because they are spiritually discerned." We must be careful not to make assumptions about God and what He wants, based on traditions of men or our personal church experiences. We must seek the Spirit of God, so that we can spiritually discern.

It grieves my spirit to think of the times I saw passionate praise dancers, including myself, told to stop moving because we were "out of order." I know this saddens the heart of God. He is the one who created and called His children to dance and move and express our love for Him. My prayer is that church leaders, rather than reacting and shutting down the joy and movement of the Spirit of God, would instead seek God's will.

God enjoys physical expressions of joy. Joy is made to be embodied. It is more than a knowing smile. The joy of the Lord is our strength (Neh 8:10b). Physical strength and joy go hand in hand. Through humble prayer, discernment, study in the word, and listening to the voice of God, He can reveal the beauty and importance of dancing in worship gatherings.

## RESTORATION OF CREATIVITY IN THE CHURCH

In Lam 5 we find a prayer for restoration. One of the qualities of the sad state of God's holy city was a lack of dancing, singing, and joy! Verses 14 and 15 (NLT) say, "The elders no longer sit in the city gates; the young men no longer dance and sing. Joy has left our hearts; our dancing has turned to mourning." I pray for the church's restoration. I pray that God will bring back more joy into our church buildings and people. I pray that He will turn mourning into joyful dancing and clothe His people with joy. I pray that we will seek His heart and that He will release a fullness of celebration into our congregations, so that we may praise and honor and glorify Him for all that He is. *For you, O Lord, are worthy to receive all glory, all honor, and all praise expression for ever and ever. Amen.*

Lest I be misunderstood, and of course this will happen in some cases either way, I am not saying that there is no joy in our modern North American churches today. I am saying that there is more joy and expression and freedom and creativity and glory for God available to us that we are not yet accessing. I am saying there is both a holding back as well as a lack of knowledge and education in our churches. We are singing with some joy, but it is a sort of "through a glass" version. It is the best we know. We are painting with blue and yellow, but we have yet to discover or paint with purple, flamingo, teal, opal, ruby, and onyx. Some feel suppressed, while others are unaware that they could open up further to the pleasure of God's presence. In both types, there is more release and fulfillment and glory and encouragement available. This freedom is our birth right, and inheritance. This is what I'm fighting for.

The struggle is real. During corporate worship services, some of us are truly, spiritually distracted; focusing on trying not to be a "distraction" or wondering if we're being "too joyful," rather than just fixing our eyes on Jesus and enjoying being with Him. This is where, I believe, leadership has a responsibility to both teach the Scriptures regarding praise and verbally encourage the congregation. God's people aren't being led well in this area. In most of our churches today, we only hear people passing around ideas like "distraction" and "causing a brother to stumble," but we are lacking solid teaching from the pulpit in this area. It becomes easy for a churchgoer to become discouraged and frustrated, not feeling welcome and confused about what's allowed and how God even feels about it. This has been my story.

I remember the first time I was chided for bringing up the value of this topic. "Keep the main thing the main thing," the pastor commanded. In a different way than he meant this, I agree. Whether at a worship service or in heaven for all eternity, the main thing is, and will always be, praising the King. Our focus should be on deepening our intimacy with Him, not moderating others' love expressions. Our goal in times of worship can be boiled down to this: connect with Jesus, and follow Him. Let him lead in your heart and body and in those of the other Christians around you.

## PAPA'S PLAYGROUND

Leave a child in a room with Legos, or the box they came in, and you can watch their imagination at play. Children are so lighthearted. They love to play. If we are to become like little children in our expression, creativity, and playfulness, let us ask: what would that look like, when we gather in our Daddy's house?

Can you see it? Papa's playground. There are two rambunctious boys swinging higher and higher. Three girls are chatting with each other on a park bench. A little boy, all by himself, is writing a poem. A group of kids are racing, enjoying the breeze in their hair. Another is dancing. Another is mimicking the bird noise in a tree. Another is laughing. Another is singing loudly and off-key. This is meant to be a space for exploration in His presence. When the saints gather at a worship or praise service, it should be a safe place to discover new aspects of God and respond to Him honestly and creatively.

# IV. WEIRD

## GOD IS WEIRD

Weird means "strikingly odd or unusual, suggestive of the supernatural, unearthly" (American Heritage Dictionary of the English Language).[1] Well, God is definitely "supernatural," but He is also weird in that he is different. William Cowper's poem "Light Shining out of Darkness" begins, "God moves in a mysterious way."[2] He is unlike others and often works in a strange, unexpected fashion.

Other gods require people to do good deeds to attempt to earn their way to heaven. Our God gives salvation as a gift that requires nothing in return; no strings attached. Other gods say, "suffer, work, pay, be less than." Our God says, "I love you. I want you. Be lifted up with Me." Our God is about unity, while other gods are about separation. Through Jesus Christ, we have direct access to God. We don't have to go through a priest or a preacher to reach God. He is present. God is always with us.

God is misunderstood. People have false religious ideas about who God is. Often, this idea of a punishing, distant God comes from being hurt by communities that preach a guilt inducing God. It's so sad that these painful experiences cause people to reject the one, true, loving God. God wants people to know Him and

1. "Weird," The American Heritage Dictionary of the English Language, https://ahdictionary.com/word/search.html?q=weird.

2. William Cowper, "Light Shining Out of Darkness," Poetry Foundation, https://www.poetryfoundation.org/poems/44028/light-shining-out-of-darkness.

understand that He is kind and gentle and full of unconditional love for them.

He sees us as His little creations and, more intimately, His own children. When religious thought and false stereotypes get in the way of people seeing Him for who He is, God gets misunderstood and rejected. I wrote this book to show you a better picture of who He is. Now we see dimly, as through glass, then we shall see Him face to face (1 Cor 13:12).

## EMBRACE YOUR WEIRDNESS

If God is weird and different, let me break it to ya friends, so are we! As His children, created in His image, we are also different, rare and spectacular. In 1 Pet 2:9 (KJV) believers are referred to as a "peculiar people." It's probably not a surprise that if you are going to be shining and reflecting a big God, you are going to stick out in this world in big ways. All His kids are at least a little odd and that's a good thing! We are conduits of the heavenly, the supernatural, on this natural earth. We were never created to act natural or normal. A Christian is not a natural woman or man, we are spiritual beings.

We are "supernatural," which means *we extra*. We're special, not regular. We are of and from a different realm. We are foreigners and aliens—strange and outlandish. What I'm getting at is, we are made to be odd. We are intended to stick out.

## BRING THE WEIRDOS BACK TO CHURCH

Art and creativity have faded out of our churches. Because these expressions of praise are unpredictable, and ultimately uncontrollable, they are labeled "out of order" and "indecent." Creative expressions are shut down, not welcomed, and told to stay in their seats. They are looked at like they're crazy, or worse that they are disrespectful of God and the church service.

Being misunderstood and rejected for being who you are hurts. When I'm giving God my all, vulnerably expressing my love and passion, and some churchgoer snaps her head around with a judgmental glare as if to say, "Not another yelp out of you, missy. This is God's house," it's so painful. My heart drops to my stomach. My eyes water and look up.

Perhaps the worst way to be misunderstood is to be perceived as being against what you are strongly for; or in this instance "who." I am for God, not against Him. I am not jumping and dancing to get attention, or whatever else may be thought, but out of a submissive, sacrificial obedience to Him. I really don't want the attention of man. It's difficult to be seen. Often, being seen leads to being judged. But God has called us to be seen to shine bright for His pleasure and glory. So, I get to move forward in faith. Even though it's difficult, I get to choose His approval over man's.

It is so much easier just to quit. Because many expressions of art and creativity, that God designed us for, are not accepted in most North American churches, many creatives go elsewhere. Lots of my lovely weirdo siblings have scattered. We go to ecstatic dances, yoga studios, other countries, drum circles, and other more welcoming settings. We find places where our oddness is welcomed, accepted, and even celebrated (as it should be in the church). We pursue safe spaces, where we can be who we are without fear or judgement.

Many artist-types even give up on the one true God, because we have been rejected by the church. Many are drawn to eastern religions and philosophies because Christian churches aren't welcoming them. I long for a church environment where creatives are safe to explore in God's presence; places where our gifts can grow and flourish for the glory of God.

Like children, the special and odd are close to God's heart. We are part of His order. We are light bearers in a unique and vital way. Yes, we stand out. Yes, we are unpredictable and seemingly uncontrollable, but so is the Spirit of God inside of us. He was, and we are, never meant to be controlled. I have seen and experienced beautiful reflections of God's heart shut down and suppressed in church. During these "worship services," childlike worship is silenced, because of its creativity and visibility. But, God created us to *shine*.

I stand for creative freedom. The Bible tells us, "Where the Spirit of the Lord, is there is freedom" (2 Cor 3:17b). When Christ's well-intentioned followers try to keep us away from His presence, Jesus says, "Let the little children come to Me, and do not hinder them." Do not try to stop them. Don't shut them down. Don't keep them from enjoying my presence. Don't try to turn down their joy, "for the Kingdom of Heaven belongs to such as these" (Matt 19:14 NIV).

# V. AUTHENTIC

## EMOTIONAL HONESTY

We live in a culture where honesty leads to rejection. Crying or feeling emotions other than chipperness and positivity leads to being labeled a "Debbie downer." We suppress our deepest thoughts, struggles, fears, and feelings, believing the lie society has taught us: "you are too much."

This sick and destructive way of "living," carries into our church culture. Church attendees feel they cannot be real, open, and honest or they will be judged and shamed. Pastors often hide, too, to keep their jobs. They often cover their despair, affairs, addictions, and feelings of desperation, because they have been put on an unhealthy pedestal. Many church leaders are the ultimate hidden ones, leading us to do the same.

I believe God has better things for us. He came to give us life abundantly (John 10:10b). Jesus was emotionally expressive. He wept. He got angry. He felt joy. He expressed those feelings and doing so was not a sin.

Many churches are infested with shame. I long for a church culture of emotional honesty. The way we can help to heal the broken and set captives free is through being honest with each other in an atmosphere of Christ-love and acceptance. "There is therefore now no condemnation for those who are in Christ Jesus" (Rom 8:1). No more shame.

## AUTHENTIC RESPONSE

Our praises should be an authentic response to Him. We are to "praise Him according to His excellent greatness" (Ps 150:2b). To respond to Him in praise and live in an appropriate way, we must look past our traditions, church experiences, cultural norms, and even family examples and consider God's heart.

The Bible says that "the heavens declare the glory of God, and the sky above proclaims His handiwork" (Ps 19:1). Indeed, all of creation reveals and displays His aspects, beauty, and attributes. We, as God's preeminent work of creativity, ought to be the most spectacular and clearest reflections of who God is. Are we being "little Christs in this world?" Are we living abundantly as "salt and light," "aliens/foreigners," "cities on a hill"? Are we living fully, free from guilt, shame, condemnation, and fear of others?

God wants us. He desires our hearts to be in relationship with Him. That means if he gives us a present, He wants to see our excitement when we open His gift, like any parent would. He's not like, "Here you go. Yes, it's the most amazing gift. It's a game changer. Just don't get too excited when you open it. Yeah, hold your joy in, in my presence, please."

God's not like some fictional girlfriend who tells her boyfriend, "Yeah, I know you're seemingly really happy to discover who I am and get to know me, just um, don't tell anyone or get excited about it. Don't even tell me how much you're enjoying getting to know me. That would be weird." Sounds sad and kind of funny, and yet that's how we live. That's how we worship and praise God.

Somewhere in our Christian history we picked up the lie that it was good for us to suppress our excitement and joy. We carry with us the regurgitated message that our authentic joy is a "distraction," that it's bad for our brothers and sisters to see or be around. If that isn't a lie from the pit of hell, I don't know what is! How can our honest displays of His glory be outlawed? How can our authentic responses of joy and adoration for Him be bad? When did our reflecting His character and shining for Him become a distraction?

# VI. DANCE

## GOD AS DANCER

Did you know that God is a dancer? This is something they're not teaching in churches. The Hebrew word *Guwl*, means to "spin around under the influence of violent emotion"; that emotion being joy![1] This idea is translated into English as the word "rejoice," but we lost much of the meaning when it was simplified from the Hebrew. We need to go to these original meanings to understand what "rejoicing" and "praise" actually are; and there are different expressions of these concepts, different Hebrew words, that are all just labeled with the same couple of English words. I have found many different forms of praise and worship when studying the Bible in its original language; and almost all of them include physical engagement.

I have no formal training in Hebrew and simply used an interlinear Bible and *Strong's Exhaustive Concordance* to research and study God's word. You can do the same. Essentially, an interlinear Bible has the English text right beside the original languages, with reference numbers above the Hebrew or Greek words. These numbers can be looked up in *Strong's Exhaustive Concordance* for a deeper understanding of each word or concept. I know sometimes it feels like only the chosen frozen can present His word, but we truly don't need a pastor to spoon feed us. Man

---

1. James Strong, "New Strong's Concise Dictionary of the Words in the Hebrew Bible with their Renderings in the King James Version," in *The New Strong's Exhaustive Concordance of the Bible* (Nashville: Thomas Nelson, 2010), 27.

ought not live on Sunday sermons alone; and few preachers even get into the Greek and Hebrew anyway. We are responsible for our spiritual growth and education. Help us Lord to be faithful in our pursuit of You. Help us to grow into our delight of You as we respond to your word.

God delights in us exuberantly. Yes, He shows us how it's done. He always loves on us first and one of the ways He expresses His affection is with physical movement (1 John 4:19). *Guwl* is what God is doing over us when He's rejoicing in Zeph 3:17. Simultaneously, He's making creative vocal expressions, which are more like ringing cries or joyous squeals than the "singing," as it's poorly translated. This type of shout of gladness is the word *Rinnah* and it is triumphant.[2] We know God better when we visualize Him twirling over us in a revolution of joy, creaking shrill pleasure sounds.

Wow! It is essential that we look to the original meanings of translated words like "rejoice" and "praise" if we want to understand God's heart for praise expression. Learning about what praise is from its original Hebrew also gave me more permission to get wild and free in expressing my feelings for our good, good God; because I see Him leading by passionate example.

## EXPLORATIVE EXPRESSION

Maybe you feel like you aren't a "dancer" or that's just not your expression. For years, I didn't think I was a visual artist. "I can't do art," I would often say. My brothers and sisters were excellent at sketching. Their art was realistic and classically based. Since that kind of detailed drawing was not something that came easily to me, I assumed I wasn't capable of art. Because I compared my potential expression to theirs, I suppressed the unique art inside of myself.

One day, I tried abstract painting and I fell in love. See, I didn't realize how broad and wide the genre of visual art was. My

2. Strong, "New Strong's Concise Dictionary," 133.

style of art is more like the driving range than putting, but it is no less valid of an expression than those of my gifted siblings.

These kinds of restricting assumptions can happen in the church too. Many churches, if they allow dance at all, have only choreographed dance. This prerehearsed dancing usually looks like a large group of trained ballet dancers, moving in sync. This is a beautiful thing, and God loves and uses formal dance training and choreography in the church to minister to those watching, but it is not the only form of dance expression that He has for us. Often, there's not a lot of congregational dancing or movement taking place because people feel like that's the role of the trained dancers. "The church already has dancers. I'm not a young, female ballerina. That must be their role," they might think. This is a sad misconception that I believe many in our congregations hold. And since, unfortunately, there isn't much teaching on praise expression (what it is, who it's for, etc.), many churchgoers are left to their assumptions.

Pastors occasionally preach about how we are commanded to sing unto the Lord; whether we feel particularly comfortable doing so or not, or think we are good singers or not. Dance is really the same type of thing. Singing and dancing go hand in hand. We are called to move our bodies, and raise our voices, for the glory of God and to respond to Him with praise. The difference between these two God-pleasing praise expressions is that one is welcomed and encouraged in the church and the other is currently outlawed. Both forms of praise, singing and dancing, are good and bring pleasure and glory to God.

## VARIETY

When, rarely, we do find dancing in the church, it's usually balletic. While ballet and classically influenced dance are lovely expressions, they are not the only Godly dance forms! They paint so lovely with blacks and pinks, but there is lavender, wild orange, fuchsia, magenta, teal, burgundy, olive, ivory, and more colors for us to explore. I long for God to receive all His glory, through different forms of movement. If we limit church dance to only trained ballet movements, we are cutting off other creative forms that are also glorifying to God and part of His plan for our church worship. That would be like saying, "Okay, only the worship team of classically, trained singers are allowed to sing. Yes, they will minister to us with their mad skills, the rest of us, hush, we aren't singers."

In this limiting perspective of church dance, we are also blocking a large group of people. There are many who, though they don't feel particularly called to ballet training, would be open to spontaneously responding to God with their bodies, if encouraged. If we only have choreographed dance in church, then we are not releasing all the beautiful, God-glorifying improvisational movement that God has for His people. We are not letting congregants learn to flow in the moment, in His presence. Much of praise movement is not meant to be practiced and rehearsed; rather it is meant to be a spontaneous response to Holy Spirit. Praise and worship isn't about being a "dancer" or a "singer." It's about making "a joyful noise," responding with what we have (Ps 100:1). We are called to respond, with our own bodies and voices, to the Lord's greatness.

It is good for churches to grow and expand in a wide variety of unique and diverse expressions of dance and movement, as well as visual art, poetry, and other creative writing forms, drama, and more. I encourage you to try. Experiment with visual art, music, pottery. Explore movement. Find your expression. You can begin in the privacy of your own home, with God. This is such an intimate and loving setting. Perhaps you want to dim the lights, play some worship music, light candles, and move. Maybe you choose to grab a coloring book and enjoy playing with colors while you pray or meditate on a scripture.

Possibly you want to pick up an instrument you dabble with and use it to commune with God in a new, prayerful way. The possibilities are literally endless, and eternal, just like our God who created creativity. You have nothing to lose, but everything to gain!

# VII. SHINE

## GOD IS LIGHT

Before God created the heavens and the earth, He created light. "Let there be light," He spoke "and there was light" (Gen 1:3). I believe God wants this same, eternal light to shine in our churches. He is saying, "Let there be light" again. Will we allow it? Will we let there be light in our bodies, praises and congregations? Will we welcome His light?

First John 1:5 (NLT) says, "This is the message we heard from Jesus and now declare to you: God is light, and there is no darkness in him at all." There is no suppression, no fakeness, no fadedness, no lack of, no less than, no condemnation, no fear in His light. God is light. We are lighted up in Him.

In John 8, Jesus calls Himself, "The light of the world" (v. 12). Psalm 119:105 reveals how growing in the knowledge of the glory of the Lord through reading the Bible gives us light when David writes, "Your Word is a lamp to my feet and a light to my path." Psalm 119:130 says, "The unfolding of your words gives light, it imparts understanding to the simple." Let us be seekers of light and truth. There is, perhaps, no better verse to illustrate God as light than this beautiful piece from Revelation: "And the city has no need of the sun or the moon to shine on it, for the glory of God gives it light and its lamp is the Lamb" (Rev 21:23).

We were created to shine not only in our churches, but in public places. Matthew 5:14-16 (NKJV) speaks to this concept of letting the light of God shine through us, "You are the light of the world. A city that is set on a hill cannot be hidden. Nor do they light a lamp and put it under a basket, but on a lampstand, and it gives light to all who are in the house. Let your light so shine before men, that they may see your good works and glorify your Father in heaven." The word "works" in *Thayer's Greek–English Lexicon* is defined as, "anything accomplished by hand, art, industry, or mind."[1] So, "good works" aren't limited to traditionally obvious forms, such as serving food at a soup kitchen; though that can certainly be a good work that shines for the glory of God. Good deeds can also be good creative works. These works can be acts of praise expression.

We are instructed to be on display for the glory of God. Dancers and creative praisers do not belong hidden in the back of the church. They are to be visible. Our loud, diverse expressions are to be seen by others, so that we can give light to everyone in the house of the Lord. And when we are seen, the praise and glory to God is compounded. Those who look on respond by glorifying God in new ways: seeing Him in a new light, through our expressions of worship. *How good you are Lord, that we don't have to hide who we are before you, in our places of worship. We are there to praise and glorify you. We are there to release into the atmosphere your essence, the Godlikeness in us.* When we release and move in who we are created to be, we declare the glory of God Himself.

When church leaders limit the types of candles allowed, or the length of the wick or the colors of candles or the height of the candle sticks, they unknowingly limit the light of God displayed in the church. They limit the encouragement that brightness could bring to those in the congregation. They limit the testimonies of light that those visiting the church might have experienced—the aliveness and celebration of God. They limit the glory of God, the glory due to His name.

My friends, let us be on the side of light. Let us choose to shine out, even in places of comparable darkness. Our churches should be lighthouses, filled with the light and glory of God. They

1. "Ergon," Bible Hub, https://biblehub.com/greek/2041.htm.

should be places that call out and attract the word, like little moths, to us. They should not just mimic rock concerts, they should not put God in a box, they should not put his people under bushels, they should not play God and regulate expressions of praise. We don't have to guess and make up rules based on fears of "going too far." There is no "too far" in God! What beauty in this truth. There is no line that is "too much." God is greater and brighter and wilder and more creative than all these lines. He is where our glory resides. He is the source of our creativity and childlikeness. "Holy, holy, holy is the Lord Almighty. The whole earth is full of his glory" (Isa 6:3 NIV).

## BEING SEEN

It is necessary for us to be seen, for God to receive maximum glory. It is one thing for us to be creative and free and expressive inside our houses; and while God does receive some glory for that, we were made for more. We were made for others too. We were created to be part of a community, using our beautiful gifts of creativity and expression to encourage, and help bring healing and comfort and passion for Christ to our brothers and sisters in God and to those who don't know God yet. How can we practice being brave or powerful if our days are relatively easy? We build our courage muscles in the presence of fear.

Dancing down the aisles at church can be very scary, because we don't know if we are going to be accepted. We don't know if our most beautiful, vulnerable pieces will be treasured and celebrated or judged and rejected. This honesty of expression takes sacrifice and great obedience to walk in bravely. When we display His light, we shine. When we shine, we stick out. It's really that simple. It is now that we come to the next question, are you willing to stand out? Are you willing to be seen? Are you willing to be called prideful or full or yourself or a show-off? Are you willing to be misunderstood? Are you willing to put honoring God above pleasing others?

# VII. SHINE

## PRIDE VS. GODLY CONFIDENCE

Our church today is guided by fears of all kinds. One of those is the fear of pride. Because people are so afraid of being prideful or even being perceived as prideful, we lower our heads. Many of our churches today breed cultures of shame. They are environments that say, "If you are honest, you will be judged. Cover up. Hide who you really are. We are in church after all." This kind of atmosphere is supported by misunderstanding the difference between the confidence of God and actual pride. Many churches have thrown the baby out with the bath water, rejecting anything that appears too big. But as we reflect God, we show a big image. We are joining with Him, and the qualities of God are awesome and vivid and spectacular. They think anything too shiny is vanity. They think if one celebrates who they are in God that is somehow taking away the glory of God.

We were not created to hide our light. We were created to shine and display His light for all to see. We must stand in the truth of who we are in Him. We bring Him glory through being who we are. We are His candles, His glory on display. When we know who we are in Him and walk in His authority, power and confidence, we are strong. Like so much in our Christian faith, this area too, is about the heart. If you judge someone based on their outward appearance, as many do, you will often misjudge and potentially suppress something that is good.

I stand for creative love. The most loving thing I can do for and unto the brother and sister praising God to my left and right is to connect with Jesus and respond to Him. The most loving thing I can do is be who He made me. It's really quite simple, connect to Jesus (the Vine) and respond to Him. Be with Him. Abide in Him.

Isn't that lovely? In this simplicity, you don't have to read minds: "Hmm, is this too much for that guy? What about that lady? If I shout out in joy, will that be too much for her?" There is no way to know what each person potentially needs. It is very possible that what they truly "need" is to see the vibrant light and joy of God in you. We cannot assume that we know best, that we know what they need. When we think of it in terms of controlling others' responses or being responsible for their reactions, we play God.

When all we are responsible to do is be with Him and let Him handle the rest. Let Him handle the person who walks in the door for the first time. Why do we assume seeing expressive praise will be bad for them? Why do we assume they will be scared and run away and never come back? Why do we assume our excitement will be a deterrent to the gospel? These are dangerous assumptions to make, friends.

Our praise expression is an evangelistic tool. In the process of evangelism, which is what our worship can be to the unbeliever, we plant seeds. We do not know how God is working in each person's heart, but we do know that the Word (made flesh) in and through us will not return void. God will use our expression and joy and light to reveal who He is and draw others to Him.

The Bible is full of examples of how this kind of God-light is used to further His kingdom and spread the gospel. Of course, when sharing God with others there will be times when people will reject Him. Some of those people come back later because of that initial seed. And sadly, some will reject Christ permanently. Thank You, Jesus, that we aren't responsible to save them, we are only called to shine His light and declare the glory of God.

Second Corinthians 4:3-6 speaks to these truths: "And even if our gospel is veiled, it is veiled to those who are perishing. In their case the god of this world has blinded the minds of the unbelievers, to keep them from seeing the light of the gospel of the glory of Christ, who is the image of God. For what we proclaim is not ourselves but Jesus Christ as Lord, with ourselves as your servants for Jesus' sake. For God, who said, 'Light shall shine out of darkness,' has shown in our hearts to give the light of the knowledge of the glory of God in the face of Jesus Christ."

Several times so far in this book, I have referred to the reality that when you connect with the holy wildness of the Holy Spirit, you will be misunderstood by some. Those who do not have spiritual eyes to see Christ in you will look at just the concrete world and will make assumptions based on what they have seen with their physical eyes. I want to comfort you with this truth: Jesus, who is the image of God, was also misunderstood and rejected on this earth. He was God and yet the religious leaders thought He was too free, too full of Himself, too wild, and too much of a rule breaker. See, Jesus disrupted the religious system of His day. He associated Himself with God directly. He came into the world so full of truth, joy and the light of God, and it was too much for those religious minds that thought they understood God based on Old Testament law. He came to fulfill the law and bring us into a new way of living: full of grace, freedom, and expressive joy!

## *SELF-LOVE*

When we understand the difference between pride, which is based on comparing ourselves to others and seeking validation through outside means, and Godly confidence, knowing who we are because of Him, we can celebrate ourselves. Knowing that we are His artwork, we are free to enjoy our bodies. We did not do the work of creating our marvelous selves, so He gets all the glory. With this perspective we are able to humbly shine; not "full of ourselves," so much as full of God. We are glorious because of God. His glory shines in us, and is what makes us wonderful. And on and on the glory of God circles. To Him and through Him be all the Glory, forever and ever (Rom 11:36).

We can bring Him honor through enjoying the gifts of our unique minds, spirits, and physical vessels. When we know that God is the source of our beauty, gifts, and power, we are at liberty to stand confidently—understanding that any celebration of who we are is a celebration of who He is and what He has created, restored and renewed in us.

In God's love, we don't have to choose between loving God, loving ourselves, and loving others. There is plenty of eternal love to go around! We don't have to choose between being lifted up, encouraging others and glorifying God. We can all rise together as we share in His joy and glory, in unity and intimacy.

We are connected. His glory is our glory. Our glory is His glory. We are glory-filled by Him. He made all of His creation glorious, reflective of His exuberant identity. When we reveal the glory, it is always His. To God be the GLORY!

# VIII. POWER

I grew up the responsible one. As the oldest of five children, I was often referred to as an example for my younger siblings. I absolutely hated getting in trouble and intensely tried to please authority figures in my life. This carried on into my teenage and adult years, as a troubling case of perfectionism, type A extremism, workaholism, and an obsession with people-pleasing. I am codependent with society, paralyzed by the possible negative reactions that others might express towards my authentic embodiment. In every space I wanted to dance, I felt I needed man's permission before I could move. This was limiting in environments like the park, or a new church setting, where I wasn't able to achieve that preapproval.

The Lord encouraged me this past Christmas with an empowering truth: we have His permission. What higher authority is there? We are approved of by the King of kings. Our dancing and authentic expressions of adoration please, and are desired by, the Lord of lords. We have permission.

Let us walk boldly then, knowing we have the permission of God. Not all pastor's hearts will be aligned with the heart of God on this. Not all church leaders will take the time to pray and search the Scriptures on these issues. Many will try to stop you or "correct" you based on them having never seen your revelation of God's creativity before or similar never being expressed in their church before. When something is unusual, people start to worry. Sometimes they feel powerless or confused. Instead of seeking God's heart through prayer and being open to His ways, they shut new expressions down. What people don't understand, they fear.

And fear leads to control. But "perfect love casts out fear" (1 John 4:18a).

This is why I long to create church environments of love and safety, where God's children can be themselves and where all His colorful expressions will be accepted and cherished.

You need no man-given title to be the leader God made you to be. It's time to run in our God-given authority and power. Nothing is impossible with God (Luke 1:37). He can do all things (Job 42:1). In Him, we walk in authority and power also. We wear His signet ring on this earth. "If God is for us, who can be against us" (Rom 8:31)?

# IX. SACRIFICE

## HUMILITY

The Scriptures refer to a "sacrifice of praise" (Heb 13:15). Often our expressive worship will be difficult. It will even hurt. It is an act of vulnerability to be on display. It is hard to obey God when others don't understand what God has called you to do. This sacrifice requires laying a body down for the good of others and for the pleasure of God. This kind of sacrifice requires humility. It takes humility to be seen, and possibly judged and misunderstood by others.

## APPEARANCES ARE DECEIVING

If someone is showing off their talents for their own glory, that can be an act of pride. If someone is on display with a heart of worship and a desire for God to be seen through them, that is good and humble. Because everything is about the heart, you could have strobe lights, a fog machine, and people clapping at the end of every song (to encourage the worship team or praise God). The scene could basically look like a rock concert and it could be totally good.

Remember, "man looks on the outward appearance, but the Lord looks on the heart" (1 Sam 16:7). Dancing, singing, shows, stages, music, drums, electric guitars, and art aren't bad in and of themselves. They are vessels: mediums which have the ability to bring honor to God or to be used for the devil's purposes. I long for a church that uses these tools, with discernment, for the good. Let us utilize all creative options available to lift Him up.

Many of our modern, North American churches have taken the lowest common denominator approach. Anything too shiny, expressive, or weird—cut it out. Unfortunately, it's not this easy. Because God Himself has aspects that are shiny, expressive, and weird. In taking this lazy approach we do a huge disservice to our congregations and our Lord. We cannot simply silence aspects of God, or His exuberant creation, because we are uncomfortable.

Instead, we need to welcome Him in His fullness, creating spaces of inclusivity for all people of God. We must create safe and open spaces for His creativity to manifest through the work of the Holy Spirit.

## MISUNDERSTOOD

To give our *Big God, Big Glory*, we must understand who we are. We are created in His image. This means we carry God with us. We are representatives and stewards of His glory. Being created in His image also means that we share similarities with God. In this next section, we will look at how we, like God, are also joyful, creative, light, powerful, holy, and often misunderstood.

When Jesus healed the demon-oppressed man in Matt 12, the amazed people asked, "Can this be the Son of David" (v. 23)? In their simple faith they saw clearly, but the religious leaders quickly "corrected them" saying that this power was of and from the devil.

"He came to his own and His own people did not receive Him" (John 1:11). The prophecy about the coming Messiah foretold in Isa 53 told that he would be "despised and rejected by men" (v. 3). Even with all His love, miracles, and divinity, the religious leaders did not recognize Him. And the other sheep in the church were too fickle to be convinced. He didn't line up with the church's idea of who God was and so they rejected the one, true God. Some did have eyes to see that He was indeed the Son of David, the Messiah, the Lord of lords, but the rest misunderstood and condemned Him.

When He was finally put to death, it was because the Jews accused Him of claiming to be a king. The idea of Him having the authority of God was a threat to their earthly regime, power, and control. When pressed, Christ honestly answered in truth, "You say rightly that I am a king. For this cause I was born, and for this cause I have come into the world" (John 18:37 NKJV). They didn't recognize their own king. They denied God because He didn't look or act like what they thought or expected.

I see this happening in our churches. We are rejecting the overflow of the Holy Spirit because it doesn't line up with our idea of what God would do and want. Let us have eyes to see spiritual realities and not forsake the expressions of God on this earth. We, God's people, are His body. We are His hands, legs, and feet on this earth, and we should let Him move freely through us.

# X. HOLY

## GOD IS HOLY

We've already discussed how God is weird. But did you know that His weirdness and holiness are connected? To be holy is to be separate, distinctly unique—to be "other" in a special way. "Who is like you, O Lord, among the gods? Who is like you, majestic in holiness, awesome in glorious deeds, doing wonders?" (Exod 15:11). "There is none holy like the Lord: for there is none besides you; there is no rock like our God" (1 Sam 2:2). Psalms 86:8-10 goes on about the distinctive holiness of God starting, "There is none like you among the gods, O Lord, nor are there any works like yours." We, His good works, are unique too; bearing the unusual mark of God.

## WE ARE HOLY

Holiness, in its more broadly known definition, has to do with purity and perfection. We are holy in this way too! Our righteousness is based on His righteousness. Our innocence on His innocence. Do you accept your holiness? If you believe in the Lord Jesus Christ and have accepted His gift of forgiveness, you are holy. You are pure now, because of what He did on your behalf. You stand in His perfection. You are a "new creation; old things have passed away; behold, all things have become new" (2 Cor 5:17 NKJV).

We can rest in this new identity, knowing that we carry the unshakable goodness of God. I challenge you to say these statements out loud: "I am holy. I am perfect. I am righteous. I am pure. I am innocent." I encourage you to do this exercise in a mirror, to really embrace these words, letting them sink deep into your identity. If you're cringing or hesitating, you might be experiencing a similar feeling to that which Simon Peter had in John 13, where Jesus was washing the disciples' feet:

> He came to Simon Peter, who said to him, "Lord, are you going to wash my feet?"
>
> Jesus replied, "You do not realize now what I am doing, but later you will understand."
>
> "No," said Peter, "you shall never wash my feet."
>
> Jesus answered, "Unless I wash you, you have no part with me."
>
> "Then, Lord," Simon Peter replied, "not just my feet but my hands and my head as well!"
>
> Jesus answered, "Those who have had a bath need only to wash their feet; their whole body is clean. And you are clean." (vv. 6-10a NIV)

It takes humility of a remarkable, unusual kind, to let the King of kings kneel and clean us. It takes true humbleness to accept such a gift; the gift of being clean. God has washed us. He has called us spotless. "What God has cleansed, no longer consider unholy" (Acts 10:15b NASB). We must accept this truth about ourselves. "There is therefore now no condemnation for those who are in Christ Jesus" (Rom 8:1a).

We are free of guilt, shame, and condemnation. It is time we lift our shameless heads and walk boldly. We carry the holiness of God. In Him, we are holy. I want to be like Simon Peter, who so fully embraced this gift of God's purification. Wash over my whole body, Jesus. You can have it all. I am yours. I accept Your goodness. I choose to believe what You say about me. Thank You, God, for my holy hands, holy feet, and holy head!

It is prideful to not accept what God says about you, assuming you know better. Pride is saying that you are not perfect, because your works aren't perfect. Do you see? Your perfection was never about anything you've done or ever could do. We are perfect because of Christ. Perfection is our identity in Him. We are heavenly beings, not earthly doings. Identity is about who we are, not what we do. God tells us, "You shall be holy, for I am holy" (1 Pet 1:16). Done, on the eternal timeline.

Our holiness is a completed deal. "It is finished" (John 19:30). It's time to accept this truth. Our actions then, rather than being based on our own human efforts to attempt to be good, are meant to flow out of our love connection with Him.

Similarly, our worship is meant to flow. Our various expressions are like plants in God's lovely garden. The church must not suffocate His worshipers, but rather let them be. Like thriving plants, God's children should all be free to grow in the light of the Son. We ought to be given space and the nourishing encouragement to move intentionally, and with ease, to the winds of His Spirit.

We can only bear the beautiful fruits of the Spirit by remaining in the Vine, in intimacy with God. Apart from Him, we can do nothing (John 15). Let us abide, for it is God that perfects us, not our own deeds, actions, and merits. "For by grace you have been saved through faith. And this is not your own doing; it is the gift of God, not a result of works, so that no one may boast" (Eph 2:8-9). So, my friends, let us "come boldly to the throne of our gracious God" (Heb 4:16 NLT); confident of our identity in Christ Jesus and His acceptance of us.

When we do so, we become emboldened to move in our unique giftings, in the purity and power entrusted to us. With our souls powerfully enriched, we can carry out the legacies God destined us for. We can "rejoice in time to come," (Prov 31:25 NKJV), knowing that He will fulfill His purpose in us. "His steadfast love endures forever" (Ps 138:8).

# PART II

## What Makes a Hero

# I. REVELATION

## FOR THE GLORY

I hope you've enjoyed learning about these lesser-known attributes of God that should both affect how we show up in the world and be responded to in praise. The second section of this book will come down from heavenly abstractions into the real world. It is filled with personal stories of how it really looks and feels to walk, and dance, these truths about God's holy wildness and creativity. What is it like to truthfully move new mind knowledge through one's limbs and throughout the physical church body?

This revelatory journey began in 2011, when I learned so much more about who God is and what He desires from us. While these insights were wonderful and exciting, I also discovered that the church at large isn't ready for this revelation. In 2013, and since, my husband and I visited many modern North American churches, only to find the pastoral teams holding steady to their limited human perspectives and traditions of man. They were more committed to maintaining the status quo, and doing things their way, than they were to the Holy Spirit's leading.

It's been over ten years since this praise journey of mine began. Maybe things are shifting. God is always at work. I see a fresh zeal in Gen Z that is very encouraging. I witness their passionate worship, big hearts, and excited evangelism. It's not cool or culturally normal anymore to be a Christian, so that means that more of those who say they are Christians are genuine.

I am also encouraged by the current church exodus, strange as that may sound. While many are disheartened by this growing trend, I am hopeful because it means that others are no longer content to mindlessly attend social clubs that lack vitality, realness, and powerful purpose. As a culture, we aren't just habitually going to church anymore. Although I can acknowledge it is sad in some way, over all I see this movement as an opportunity for future restoration. This coming rebuilding may need to start with a tearing down of every stronghold that sets itself up against the knowledge of God (2 Cor 10:5). Gone is the time when we go to church to keep up with the Jones family. We aren't to be followers anyway, going along with the world and living by man's standards. We are to be consciously connected to Christ, following after Him with authenticity and the courage that journey requires.

Those moments in my journey where I left the church building brought to mind the biblical exodus. Like the Israelites, I no longer wanted to be chained down. I was willing to give up false security and limited comfort for freedom. I was willing to brave the wilderness, even if I had to do so alone with God.

Over the years, I did keep looking for a church home, because I believe we're meant to be in community. God made us with the ability to contribute to a church family through the unique gifts He entrusted to us. And I have tried, and keep trying, because I believe in the biblical concept of church. Sadly, though, over the course of ten years I have rarely found such a space of liberty and acceptance. Many other folks are also getting sick of the church coffins and refusing to be just another corpse on a pew. Maybe change is happening. Maybe He is calling us forward "for such a time as this" (Esth 4:14b). *Dear God, let it be so.*

This is the story of one hero's quest to bring God all the GLORY. This is the story of how my God is faithful through it all. He brings water and manna in the wilderness. I want to bring your attention to the thread of His loyal goodness, and who He is, an ever-present help (Ps 46:1). He never lets us go. Like Jonah discovered, we cannot hide from His love or presence. The truth is,

## I. REVELATION

He is our hiding place. He protects us from trouble. He surrounds us with songs and passionate shouts of deliverance (Ps 32:7).

## SEEKING

Just after college, I started going clubbing out of desperation. I couldn't be myself in church, but in the nightclubs people could celebrate and dance freely. Expressing emotions through the body is something I was created to do, but couldn't find a wholesome outlet anywhere else in society; certainly, not in the church.

Historical cultures had barn dances, swing dances, courtly dances, and sock hops. In 2010 America, we didn't have societal safe spaces for movement. It's sad how the church has let the devil take dance when it really comes from God. It's heartbreaking how so many of God's creative children find themselves in the twisted arms of the devil, because he provides them the illusion of acceptance and because the church is lacking in this vitally important way—similar to how one is drawn to Eastern religions because the Christian church isn't teaching Sabbath rest. So, we get our temporary fill in a counterfeit the devil excitedly provides.

My chapter in the world didn't end well. Those chapters never do. The devil lured me in with a promise to fulfill the desires of my heart, my God-given longing to dance with people in freedom. He knew I needed this and was made for it. So, he baited the hook of destructive sin with the juicy liberty I longed for and I bit hard. I was so hungry for freedom of expression. I was starving for acceptance; to be seen and known and celebrated for who I truly am.

I was every bouncer's favorite, surely because I carried the light of God into those dark spaces. At first, I was extra bright and shiny with the Spirit of God. I even stepped outside with people to share Christ with them, but I didn't belong in nightclubs. I was made to dance in God's house; safe, beloved and secure.

## A REVOLUTIONARY EXPERIENCE

In the spring of 2011, I attended a conference on creativity in Lakeland. They spoke of how we can praise God through visual art, creative writing, dance, drama, improvised music, and more! My ears were buzzing. I felt like I was getting to know a gorgeous, radiant piece of God's heart that Satan, through a misguided church, had kept hidden from me.

Hidden. That's just where Satan wants our light, under a bushel. And that's the lie that prevails in our modern North American churches. We believe we are holier when we are quieter. Whether joy or sadness, we hide our honest displays of emotion from God and from each other. In most of our church services today, the less creative and unique we are the more "appropriate" we are. But this is a lie. God made us creative, expressive, and unique.

At the weekend workshop, a long-bearded man leading worship pointed right to me and called, "Come forth daughter. Come forth and dance!" It was the weirdest moment of my life, but it didn't take two seconds for me to jump out of my seat and step into my calling. Dancing before the Lord felt so good, freeing, and right. I was finally free to be the expressive girl He made me to be. But in my mind, I was harboring the fear of being a "distraction."

In my previous church experiences, I had been told by church leaders that I must focus on not taking attention away from God. I didn't want to be selfish. I didn't want to cause my brother to stumble. I was confused. Dancing seemed to be okay here, but why? After worship time, I was worried. I had done something that went against what I had been taught. Did I do something wrong? My head was lowered and I was torn inside.

Surprisingly, people started to come over to me. "Thank you so much for your beautiful worship." "Wow," one teary-eyed old man beamed, "when you danced, something broke off me. Some burden, some barrier. I feel free." These were not the words I expected to hear, words of condemnation and disapproval. Instead, people were thanking me for my joyful expression of praise. Ministry, healing, and encouragement took place through me just being myself in His presence and enjoying Jesus. My spiritual eyes were opened wide that day. Maybe I was not made to be hidden. Maybe it was good for people to see me dance.

At this conference, I was also introduced to the Hebrew words for praise—the concept that "praise" is an English word and we must look it up in the Hebrew when we find it in Scripture to understand it's true meaning. We lose depth and accuracy by neglecting to look at the original words and their meanings. There are many different, powerful Hebrew words that have all been translated into just "praise" or "rejoice" in English. I was surprised and encouraged to learn that most of these words that define what praise really is, include a physical component. Our bodies are meant to join in praising God!

# II. EXPLORATION

## PROCESSING

I had a lot to think about as I went back to my little Baptist church home: a place that taught that God is glorified through our sameness. Now the four walls of that place felt thick and heavy. I wanted to do more to express my affection for God than just sing. I knew now, what was inside me all along, that people aren't all the same and our expressions are diverse. I didn't know what to do with this new knowledge. They said if you are a creative freak, if you are different from how a godly one should be, at least try to calm down. Don't go "too crazy" and try to blend in so you're not a distraction.

"Distraction," I have seen this word used possibly more than any other to suppress the joy of God in His children. It is a dangerous word. It comes out of the mouths of some with good intentions, but it is not from God. The concept of passionate praise being a distraction is not biblical. It is based on the fear of man, tradition, control, and comfort zones, not on God's heart. At that time, I felt so suppressed. I knew God wanted all of me. He wanted not just my mind and heart but also my body in worship.

I know now that connecting with Christ and obeying Him in praise expression, letting Him lead in worship, is so right! It's what He wants and made us for! Expressive praise isn't a distraction; it's a display of His glory, a revelation of Him that is good for people to see! We, as His creations, are called to declare the glory of God, even though some might misjudge us.

## II. EXPLORATION

Exuberant David's own wife judged him for his free expression (2 Sam 6:16). She was in the wrong for despising him in her heart. We are not to call impure that which God has said is good (Acts 10:15). It is best to pray and listen for wisdom rather than reactively jump to judgement.

## WEDDING

In 2013, my Michael and I got married. The ceremony took place in our cousin's backyard on a lake. I sang my vows, even though everyone warned me I'd be too nervous. We hired a teenage folk duo to play our reception. There were picnic blankets spread across the lawn. The groom wore shorts, though some family members didn't approve. As I look back, I can see in myself a righteous rebel who makes authentic choices not based on the expectations or preferences of others. *Lord, help me to be who You've created me to be.*

My ninety-five-year-old great-aunt GrandMary flew to our wedding. She has prayed for me and been my pen pal for over twenty years. Fifteen minutes before the ceremony, she took a swim in the backyard pool—the glory of her white hair sweeping the floating yellow lanterns.

## EAST COAST WORSHIP TOUR

In the summer of 2014, my husband was awarded an architectural travel scholarship. We went up the east coast from Florida to New York, visiting some of the world's most memorable and splendid structures. I took the opportunity as a praise exploration trip. I wanted to study the subject of praise and worship more deeply. I wanted to see if there were others who were aware of the meanings of praise in the Hebrew language and were expressing creativity in worship. Maybe I wasn't alone.

As we poked inside large cathedrals I would sing. The well-formed acoustics made my voice echo and divinely resonate.

I communed with God in St. Paul's by the Sea in Jacksonville, Cannon Chapel in Atlanta, and St. Patrick's Cathedral in New York City. God gave me a gift in the Cannon Chapel. On one of the pews was a book titled *Creative Ways to Praise*. I felt like this was a confirmation of my journey, like I was on the right path.

During our hours on the road, we listened to my mentor Ray Hughes. I met him once (at the Lakeland conference). He is a kind-hearted, rugged sort of cowboy historian with a mind for revival history, sound, and God's heart for worship. He is a comedian storyteller with a poet's soul.

I'm sure the families we stayed with on our trip were arranged by God. We stayed up late picking each other's brains about the heart of God and plucking through questions on the topic of praise and expression. They seemed to have ears to hear, and I was so encouraged.

One Sunday, we were right beside Morning Star Ministries— a worship hub in the Carolinas. We showed up to find they were on a summer hiatus. Thankfully our disappointment was lit by hope. A man there invited us to his church—a small chapel with white wood panels and loud singing. As we came in, we saw a man pacing up at the front of the church—movement in worship! This man was helping to lead people into worship from the congregation; something I'd never seen! "Come on," he would shout, "let's give God his glory" or "somebody give a shout for God in here." He was supporting the worship leader, who was on the platform. They were working together. When the preaching began, they sat side by side. Unified in their purpose. Marvelous.

I love the idea of leaders in the congregation helping bring Spirit-filled movement and life into the atmosphere. The "big man" on stage wasn't threatened by this man's passion. He was encouraged by it. What a powerful idea. This kind of teamwork works well. I thought of all the blocks against this kind of pairing in our churches—pride, fear, control, newness. I am a congregational leader type myself. I, too, lead from the crowd, helping others around me to come forth, release, and praise Him bountifully.

As the service continued, a young woman came up and sang, then went right into teaching. Then another used her exuberant wit, sense of humor and personality to deliver the most creative sermon I've ever heard. Following her were three dancers interpreting a majestic gospel hymn with movement—spurning on profuse shouts, hand swaying, and claps of praise. Then a group of children came up to prophesy. One little boy said to me three words I'll never forget: "Move the mountains."

This church felt good. I didn't want to go back to the frozen hard iceboxes back home. There isn't warmth there. I wanted to stay in this flowing waterfall. I wanted to be by a freshwater spring like this. I must be free. After the service, a woman told me that she saw a rainbow over my head while I was worshiping. "Beams of light were coming down over you. God is pleased with your worship."

After our summer trip, I went back to the Lakeland church, where I had attended the creativity conference, for praise jams. I would bring my viola and singing voice and we would improvise together in the spirit of God. Once after dancing there, the assistant pastor encouraged me, "When you dance you release something powerful and freeing into the atmosphere." His father, the head pastor, added that he was happy to have me using my gifts at his church. I had never been encouraged in these ways. God was building me up. He was speaking to me through his people. God was fanning my flame into a roaring fire.

# III. CHURCH

## *AN UPLIFTING EXPERIENCE*

My brother attended a church in South Florida that had dancing. We would later attend this church regularly for multiple years. When I visited, a little man in the front row told me, "You're a jumper and a dancer. You're going to jump over obstacles and crush walls under your feet." After whispering this to me, he got up on the platform and began to preach. This was a church that welcomed spirit-led physical praise expression. They even had a dance ministry.

God was opening my eyes. He was showing me that there are various kinds of people out there, diverse types of Christians in the world. His kids can be creative and accepting and open. I think today how blessed I am by the encouraging words I've received along my journey; words that have impacted who I am, who I'm growing to be. Sometimes I want to be discouraged by how hard this journey has been. It is so good to look back to see the lights shining on my path.

When I got back to St. Petersburg, Florida, my husband and I visited churches in the area. We weren't too picky with exact doctrine, style of music, age of congregants or much else; we just needed a place that believed that salvation is through Jesus Christ alone, and that would let me worship God freely.

## III. CHURCH

## NOT OPEN FOR CONVERSATION

At a church in Clearwater, Florida, I was told to stay in my seat because my praise was a "distraction." After the service, I attempted to begin a dialogue with a staff member. When I tried to speak about God's heart and have a conversation, I was told, "We have no choice in this. This is just how our church does it." I remember my heart racing, as I tried to decide how I should respond. He seemed so closed and powerless. I wasn't hopeful that my sharing would make any difference. I kept silent. My spirit ached. I shook the dust from my feet (Matt 10:14).

## DON'T GET TOO CRAZY

Although the church name, Limitless, was promising, it did not fulfill that promise. There were definitely limits! I was told not to get "too crazy" (whatever that means). "We want to think about others when we're worshiping," they said condescendingly. Why can't we just focus on Jesus? "We don't want to be selfish," they said, trying to teach me. It is sad that we live in a time where praising God all out and sacrificially (because it is a sacrifice to be put out on display for others, to be misunderstood and judged) is considered "selfish."

In this popular worship environment, it's impossible to know what the uncommunicated rules are. We are trained to look to the right and to the left. We compare ourselves to others, using them as the standard for what is right. Our attention should be upward, inward, and toward the pages of our Bibles, yet this fearful environment which propagates mental chaos is the standard today. One cannot know how far is "too far," so we try to mind read, guessing others' possible comfort zones. When did Jesus compromise the sacred truth of who He was to cater to others' comfort zones? The line of how much is "too much" is vague, blurry, and suppressive. Because worshipers don't know where each individual pastor's line is, they tend to tone down their expression so they won't get shut down by church leadership or judged by their fellow congregation members. They don't feel accepted and welcome to be true to who they are in that space.

Worship time can be as simple as this: *connect with Jesus.* Obviously, remain enough in the physical reality that you don't smack somebody in the head when you're twirling! Hah! But be free, there is no such thing as "too crazy" in the house of God. No such thing as "too wild" when we are following the Holy Spirit's breath and leading. He is where our order should come from, not man-based, handed down, wishy-washy rules.

We must be liberated to move as He leads, often outside of the bounds of human understanding and into heavenly mysteries. We get to be a part of bringing eternal truths to earth, of connecting divine with physical. We get to reveal and carry the glory of God.

Thank You, Jesus, for the gift of your presence. Thank You for the incredible mystery of the Holy Spirit's ways. Thank You that Your thoughts are higher than ours (Isa 55:8-9). We trust You and we surrender our wills, bodies, and human understanding (Prov 3:5-6). Help us to dance on the path You lead us on, Father, however whacky we may appear to unknowing minds. The more we connect with heaven, the more we stick out on the earth.

## MORE CLOSED MINDS

As we continued on our journey, we attended a small church with a young pastor. We bore with the congregation awhile and built relationships, but the pastor's head was blocking his heart with regard to praise expression. We went to home group, and got quite close with the pastor and his wife. We served in the child care ministry. Despite building trust, theological credibility, and personal relationships, there was still a lot of fear and restriction. When I tried to have conversations referencing the Bible, and sharing what I had learned on the topic, I came up against defensiveness.

I was finally allowed to dance, but only in the back, hidden away. My spirit was suppressed. The pastor wanted to understand everything, which of course we can't do with the mysterious ways of God. He thought I was judging his church's current worship, when I was simply telling (with Scriptures in hand and love in my heart) that there was more.

I was trying to bring awareness to the possibilities in praise for His glory. I wanted, and still want, to introduce folks to a richer vocabulary of praise. I am an advocate for diversity in praise expression, because these diverse variations on praise are according to God's taste and He deserves to receive all the expressions He created for us to worship Him with.

I wish this pastor, and the others I encountered, would've prayed and listened in silence. I wish they could've lifted their concerns up to God and sought His wisdom.

# IV. ENCOURAGEMENT

## STUDYING BIBLICAL PRAISE

I began a personal study on the Hebrew words for praise. I looked up the words "praise," "rejoice," etc. in the original language, and found quite a bit of variety in the original meanings. As I continued my research, I found forty-seven different words for praise expression! There is much more there, biblically, than raising hands, singing, and clapping. I wanted to get the word out, so I started making teaching videos and posting them online. I began connecting with ministries I thought might be interested in, or open to, what God had revealed to me about His heart for praise. He led me to some leaders who truly encouraged me and could be taught through me. I even hosted a few workshops where I taught about these biblical concepts, both physical and vocal expressions.

## MEETING A PROPHET

Coming from a cessationist background, I was skeptical and a little nervous when I first met a prophetess. I had been taught that prophets only existed in the Bible. I might have assumed she was a false prophet, had not God already opened my eyes to understanding the limitations and flaws of the doctrines I grew up with (like that of how they misunderstood how praise should be embodied in the church). I now valued truth over tradition. I was very open to the idea that God can move in whatever ways He chooses.

## IV. ENCOURAGEMENT

I also knew that the Holy Spirit wants to show up in physical manifestations, yesterday and today. That didn't change. It's who He is. The Holy Ghost is expressive, and He uses us to express Himself. This can be through a variety of expressions including teaching, Spirit-tickled laughing, physical healing, speaking in tongues, witnessing, praise dance, words of knowledge, encouragement, prophecy, and more. I want to know more about God, and am open to all of who He is, even if what I discover doesn't fit my current mental conception or is larger than my past experiences.

When the prophetess and I first connected, she said I better get my running shoes tied, "cause I'm going places," then she anointed me. She invited me to speak at her church, which turned into two marvelous hours of dancing, shouting, praying, speaking, leading, singing, and praising God. This bold and spiritually out-there woman of faith helped encourage me to move and speak and lead in freedom. At the end of this spontaneous praise time, she anointed me again, this time for my calling. She focused on my feet, for dancing and standing firm for Christ. Thank you, brave and loud woman of God.

## HOPE RESTORED

We were about to move to Fort Lauderdale for Michael's architecture studies, and had almost given up hope of finding a congregation, when God gave us a gift. While browsing on Facebook for churches, I clicked on a church featuring a video in which the pastor was inviting the viewer to coffee. He said he would gladly buy them a cup and hear their story. I had a story to tell, so I took him up on it.

We met at a little coffee shop in downtown St. Petersburg. I found him sitting outside, reading his very colorfully highlighted Bible. This pastor, like his Bible, was open and ready to receive color! He wasn't an ageist, sexist, or prideful man like many of the other pastors I'd met. He really listened to me. He wanted to hear my story, not just talk about his church or vision. I could tell he respected me as part of God's magnificent creation. He invited me to a worship night his church was having that night. He invited me to dance freely.

Michael and I began regularly attending his church. It took us almost two years to find a place wise and wild enough to welcome my wall-shattering ways. And they speedily put me to beneficial use, acknowledging me as the leader I am. I didn't have to serve time, climb ladders, and prove myself. I was seen for who I was, in the Spirit, and celebrated. I shared my poetry and played viola in the church praise band. I sang and rapped original music. After one of the services, a congregant said "Your sensitivity is beautiful. You play as if led by the Holy Spirit." I was being used, my gifts released into the atmosphere for the good of my community. This is what I was made for.

I danced down the aisles on Sunday mornings, and was given the chance to choreograph group dances. People were touched. I felt freer than ever: supported by the congregation and the pastor, and validated as a dancer worshiper. I knew the hearts of those around me and was worshiping with them like never before. There were a few young people that were inspired by my freedom and started dancing. I encouraged and supported them in their bravery. It felt wonderful to be a mother bird that puts protective wings around others to nurture and call them into their true purpose and calling. This is what that pastor did for me and what I will do for others.

## LEADING AT A CONFERENCE

That summer, while still attending that uplifting church, I saw lots of encouraging growth in my garden. I danced for a healing conference called "Journey to Freedom" and for a baby shower put on by a nonprofit that supports teen moms. I also taught a summer Bible study series about praise expression where I spoke about God's heart for diversity and freedom in our worship.

## IV. ENCOURAGEMENT

A kind female pastor welcomed me to lead a multiple night conference on the subject of deepening in our praise expression. I taught one evening on physical praise expression, and the other on vocal praise expression. These sessions were workshop style. First, I introduced a vocabulary of praise, new expressions available to explore. Then, space was provided for attendees to explore with God in a worship setting. Three sisters from a local charismatic group came to dance and lead worship. These were beautiful moments where I helped expand minds and hearts towards heaven.

Michael and I were even invited back to the church that hosted the conference to provide special music for a Passover gathering. I sang "This Little Light of Mine," while Michael played percussion. *Let it shine. Let it shine. Let it shine.*

I am so grateful to have been provided this opportunity to use my gifts to edify this special congregation. In my experience, female pastors have been more welcoming and open-minded, because similarly, they have had to come up against resistance and judgement in their own journeys.

## A JOURNEY IN MY IMAGINATION

I connected with a school of supernatural ministry in Tampa. There, I was reminded that our imagination isn't just for temptation. Our thoughts, creativity, and ability to fantasize can be redeemed and renewed. One of the leaders took us on a meditative visualization exercise, where we invited the Holy Spirit to guide us in our imaginations. First, she asked us to close our eyes, then raise a hand when we could see a gate.

When I walked through it, there was a meadow with a garden all around it. Jesus came toward me, picked me up, and hugged me. He said He had something for me. He spread His arms wide. He is my present, and the promise that He will always be with me. He was with me in worship, when I felt like I was standing all alone. He held my hand and we started running through the field. It was freeing, running with Jesus. When we got to the edge of a cliff, I was afraid. I looked up to Jesus. We started to fly.

Soaring above it all with Him, I was developing faith and an adventure's spirit. We flew to heaven to visit the Father. He was overjoyed to see me and swept me up on His lap. He threw me into the air like a baby. This made Him laugh and giggle. I laughed and giggled too as He threw me higher and higher. As He played with His baby, I realized: God wants me to laugh with Him. We had so much fun. God enjoys me so much. Then the Father started dancing and His strides were so huge. The heavens shook and trembled when His feet hit the gold ground. Power. Joy. Passion. Expression. Enthusiasm. God!

Then Father, Son and Holy Spirit joined hands and moved triumphantly in a circle. They were dancing. I stood in awe, so small. God seemed to say, "You think your movement is weird, loud and crazy? You came from me. I'm your Daddy. You were made in my image." At this He reached out His hand. He wanted me to dance with Him. God wants me to dance with Him, I thought. And I did. I twirled and circled around with my full-of-wonder God. After a while I stepped out of the circle again, in amazement.

After I watched those three dance in unison, He put out His hand again. This wasn't just a one-time thing. He loves dancing with me and wants to do so again and again. Yeah, it's kind of our thing.

I can still hear my Father laughing in that loud heavenly rumble and I know He takes good pleasure in me. I often laugh in His presence, remembering heaven, my eternal home. I lift up my eyes, tilt my head back and soak in the memory of His throne room. I see the Trinity dancing, and remember that I am invited into Their circle of perfect movement. Thank You Lord, for making dance. Thank You for your example of thunderous Joy. Thank You, that You delight in Me. Help me to delight ever deeper, in Your presence—where there is "fullness of Joy" (Ps 16:11).

## IV. ENCOURAGEMENT

### PERICHORESIS

Years after God showed me this picture, I discovered the term "Perichoresis." It is a Greek word ancient scholars used to describe God's relationship with Himself. Perichoresis, the Trinity, is a circular dance. I wasn't the only one who saw father, son and spirit dancing together in a circle. My triune God has been pictured this way for centuries. Finding that term was God confirming my vision for His praise to be set free. God is already dancing, and he wants us to move with Him, through Him, in Him. In Acts we read, "In Him we live and *move* and have our being" (17:28a).

Yes, please Lord and amen! If I ever start a church on this earth, I think its name will be "Glory House" and I think this circle in a triangle will be our symbol. Or, perhaps it will be called "House of Belonging," because I want to create a space of true acceptance. Of course, in my journey I didn't get to experience being welcomed, honored, and appreciated for all I carry. I want to provide a safe space where we can celebrate one another in our uniqueness, all while honoring and praising the giver of all good gifts. So needed in a church are the values of freedom, revolution, transformation, inclusion, wholeness, and overflowing, vibrant, glowing life.

I am still growing on this journey of creative and free expression. I have Sundays where I run, jump, and dance. Sundays where I move around the congregation and minister to people through prayer-filled, healing movement. Prayer meetings where I dance the prayers to heaven. Times where I pound rhythms on my legs as the words build on hearts or meditatively trace on the rug when we're praying about love in our church. And still Sundays, where I sit at home with God, mornings where I'm not strong enough to lace up and put on the armor.

My life consists of victories and weaker moments. What makes me strong is my will to get back up. I refuse to give up on God's bride, even though she is blind and imprisoned in many ways and has hurt me immeasurable times. God has not given up on her and, so help me God, neither will I.

So, I carry on. I try to let myself flow in the Holy Spirit. I try to give myself permission to surrender, permission to let go. I am not some superhero. Or maybe I am. Aren't they just people burdened with big, beautiful gifts, destined to be used for good?

# V. LADDER SYSTEMS AND COOL KIDS' CLUBS

## PLATFORMS AND PEDESTALS

I am in awe of the bravery and exuberance of the woman whose voice I know. The past ten years have carried more memories, experiences, and weight; including a move from Florida to New York and then (a year later) another to California before moving to Seattle. Many more conversations on the topics of praise, creativity, and liberty have been had. The same questions answered again and again like the following: "What about visitors coming in?" "Why not just dance in the back?" "Aren't we called to order in worship?" We experienced more rejections from churches because I would not stay in the back. I will not hide my light. I must follow Jesus, wherever He leads. I will not cover my God-gifted joy in a cloak of shame-filled embarrassment or human approval.

Our last year in South Florida, we left the church we were worshiping at. I had tried for over two years to offer a class alongside the current ballet class that would be a safety net to collect all those that didn't feel like they fit into the classical ballet school the church was already running. I wanted to provide a space for free-form praise exploration, to help the dance-curious of all ages and genders deepen in their journey of connecting with God in the body.

I tried to use my speaking and teaching gifts too, but there was a wall there. This church was much like a social club. It had an inner circle of cool kids who had been there since the beginning and they monopolized the teaching/speaking roles. They would often mention patience when it came to using your gifts, but I don't see this biblically, and how many years do they expect one to wait? I can't serve in the kitchen for ten years waiting to use my actual gifts.

See, they had this unbiblical perspective about the hierarchy of gifts. I guess because the praise band and speaking roles are on the platform, you had to earn your way up there. This perspective is actually propagating the pedestal mentality. Instead, the church needs to let people just use their gifts. People with platform gifts aren't better than or more valuable than people who set up for the service, run audio for worship, or cook the meals. It was discouraging to keep trying to be of service and never being able to break through the social glass ceiling. "Keep showing up. Get to know the ladies," they said; but after two years of trying to "earn my way to Heaven," I remembered that we aren't called to prove ourselves to men. I don't want to work with people who I have to suffer silently alongside for an unknown number of years while my insides sit on the shelf. I want to show up big and serve my community. I want to participate in the service, being all of who God has called me to be.

I was recently speaking to a children's ministry leader who said she didn't want volunteers who view serving in children's ministry as a stepping stone to speaking upstairs. This ministry is already valuable and perfectly aligned with someone's gift. A person who speaks to big people isn't more valid in their giftings than someone who speaks to small people. While I fully agree, I will say that it is the church that usually propagates this narrative and has set up such a system. I have been in many spaces that ask you to serve your time and prove your commitment by stacking chairs after services. Rather than valuing each gift, they set up systems where you have to do someone else's gift first before you get to do your own.

This testing and proving oneself often goes on for years. How long does one need to toil at a place outside of their giftings before they can run in who God has called them to be? Meanwhile, a person's spiritual gifts aren't being used and practiced. Suppressed and unfulfilled, they dry up on the vine. The earn it culture is one that stands in opposition to the message of salvation and the life of grace that we are meant to live. We aren't meant to be outside the inner circle in our churches, always trying unsuccessfully to be a part of the community. We have been given a seat at the table, that we don't have to earn. We are a part of the family of God, because of the work of Christ on our behalf. We are already valued members of the body.

This man-made control system, with its pedestal ideology, devalues the woman in hospitality or the man who cares for the church grounds. We should each get to serve according to our gifts, and each gift should be valued. There should not be a hierarchy system, nor should we be required to work our way up a ladder doing random things. God has called each according to their gifts, and space should be made to include each member so that we can be useful to the body in a way that God designed us.

## NEW STATE, SAME STATE

In Troy, New York (2018), we opted for a Bible study instead of a church service as we could see that the area was quite traditionally minded and stunk of stagnant structures. This worked out fairly well, though my soul craved worship with other believers. God drew me to another woman who had left the church. She was also a speaker who was frustrated about not being able to participate in the services with her special gifts. She also has similar frustrations regarding man's control over the Spirit's leading. We danced all summer to live music, sipped tea, and talked theology and in the winter gathered with a few others to praise and pray and talk about the things of God: refreshment for my soul. *Thank You, Lord.*

## KICKED OUT OF HOME GROUP

In Berkeley, California (2019/2020), I danced freely at a church for six months until one day we were informed that the pastor didn't want anyone to see bodily worship. He was afraid of visitors' perceptions and his reputation being negatively affected. Dear friends, I hope you know that church is made to be God's house—a place where He is honored and adored; a place where we lay down our pride and focus on His glory, goodness, and pleasure. The church is meant to be a space to encourage, educate, and uplift believers; not appease visitors and attempt to control their experience.

Interestingly, one guest told me that she attended the church because of my worship. "Wow, when I saw you move, I knew there must be something alive here; something real." She came from a Catholic background, and hadn't experienced any passion in the ritual. Yet, pastors often try to play God; rather than being authentic and focusing on creating inclusive spaces to worship God freely. The truth is, we don't know what God is going to use to draw people to Him. Who's to say that the very dancing the pastor feared would scare people off may not just attract them to God's light. Let's let God lead His church. Let us not stifle the Holy Spirit (1 Thess 5:19).

This shocking announcement was heartbreaking because we thought we'd found a safe place to worship. The harvest seemed ripe there, as so many of the church people were open to truth and weren't tied down by traditions. Many of them were new Christians excited to learn about who God was. I had been dancing there for six months and thought I had a family.

Oh how the devil loves to destroy a good thing. He used the tradition in the pastor's experience, fear, and pride to gain a foothold in his mind. Without praying and seeking God's heart for wisdom, he reacted out of man's reasoning and shut down the work God was doing, including a sweet older woman who God had given fresh energy and new hope through my ministry there and a sweet break-dancing guy who used to dance in the front row even before I came to the church. "I thought my life was over," the older woman exclaimed joyfully while dancing with me in the front, "but now I see it's not. I have purpose!" God was doing good things in this congregation. The people were receptive, young Christians who were encouraged through my gifts. It was sad that the devil, knowing the power and effectiveness of praise, shut down the good work God was doing in that house.

Even though we couldn't attend what became a suppressive Sunday service, we were excited that we would still have our community group. Because we didn't know anyone in the area, these folks made up our whole friend group. Outside of weekly meetings, we spent time throughout the week and even enjoyed holidays together. It was a shock when they told us we could no longer be a part of the group gatherings because we were no longer attending the Sunday service. The small group leader seemed to deliver this message with the empathy of a loyal robot.

I have seen this again and again: humans following other humans. Humans learning about God from a person and looking up to that person too much. Remember, dear ones, you can approach God directly. You can think. You can pray. You can listen to God's voice. The pastor's voice doesn't trump all. God's does. We must keep Him first, keeping our ears open to what He has to say.

## WILDERNESS

A month after we were kicked out of our home group community because I refused to conform to man's ways, instead of God's, the COVID-19 pandemic began. While groups from our recent church continued to meet and encourage each other during those confusing and difficult times, we were isolated and alone. We tried to reach out to members of our group to see if they would hang out with us. One couple was willing to hike outdoors with us, but the others were too fearful.

Additionally, Berkeley had a rule that you must have a "social bubble," and you could not hang out with more than ten people. Because we had moved to the Bay Area only six months before, and had spent all our social energy on developing and nurturing relationships with that church community, we weren't close enough friends to make anyone's "bubble," and we didn't have any friends outside of that church. Other than occasional Zoom calls with family in Florida, we were completely alone.

The beauty of this time was how God used it to deepen our dependance on Him. We couldn't rely on a pastor to spoon feed us weekly, we had to suckle directly on the Vine. Needy in the desert for substance and living water, He provided in such a tender and intimate way. In the summer of 2020, we moved from Berkeley to a town twenty minutes away, Martinez, to mix things up. There were hiking trails near our house and I would go up daily to a private place to dance and pray and worship, communing with God in nature, like Jesus did.

I connected with a couple of like-minded praise dancers on Instagram, and got to participate in their devotional dance challenges. One was around Easter. I love Easter because it's all about resurrection—coming out from burial and death and moving upward and forth into new life. It was encouraging to be seen in my gifts, and witness others who understand connecting with God in their bodies.

A couple of years after moving to Martinez, we moved again. This time, we headed to the epic nature of Marin County— debatably San Francisco Bay's most gorgeous area. Everything was shut down, and masks were required everywhere. It was suffocating, and all I wanted to do was get out into the freedom of open space. Every day I walked with God in the wilderness. He drew me so close to Himself. I was sad and lonely and so let down by people, but He has never let me down. He has never left me or forsook me (Deut 31:8).

## V. LADDER SYSTEMS AND COOL KIDS' CLUBS

In Martinez, I had set up a hammock on the top of a hill off of a steep deer trail. In Novato, I had a special prayer bench on a lake. Sweet memories were made in both of these places that I intentionally went to go away with God. Sometimes, while walking, He would beckon me to be with Him. I love soaking on a single scripture, just meditating on the goodness of God, or ingraining some principle into my spirit. Often, I would dance with Him in the privacy and beauty of our one-on-one time outside.

## NEW LAND

In December of 2022, my husband and I fasted every Sunday in order to seek God's will as to where we should go next. I was eager to leave California, after being suppressed and having my voice shut down there for three years. As we listened for God's leading, we saw evergreens and mountains. We felt drawn to the Pacific Northwest, particularly Washington state. Though the city of Seattle is quite a dark place spiritually, the surrounding lands are filled with the GLORY.

Upon moving, I sent many emails to churches, "Do you welcome physical expressions of praise? Do you allow freedom of worship? Do you welcome congregants to bring before the Lord the fullness of their being—to praise Him with mind, spirit, and body? Two responded yes! The others had disclaimers and hesitations.

We started attending one of these churches. One Sunday I ran laps around the space during, "His goodness is running after me." I high-fived one lady each time I ran around. I went to different parts of the sanctuary as I felt led. There was another woman dancing with fabrics. I felt encouraged. After worship, a woman expressed, "Your worship is so beautiful." An older woman also told me she loved watching me worship, especially the jumping. I felt encouraged to be in an environment where folks appreciated passionate expressions of love for the Lord and they weren't afraid to share what they saw. After one of the services, a prayer warrior anointed my feet for dancing and prayed for freedom.

## HAVE YOU BEEN BAPTIZED
## IN THE HOLY SPIRIT?

My story is unique because while I am very open to Holy Spirit manifestations, and believe that God can heal and speak and move through us today, I am still from an Evangelical Baptist background. I go to churches where folks have some different doctrinal differences and yet I happily coexist because I am grateful for the free worship environment. The way I see it, we will all be in heaven someday worshiping together if we're trusting in Jesus Christ alone. I have no problem starting that heavenly scenario of diversity in unity, now.

Unfortunately, this is another little box that folks fixate on— those who have the luxury of a denomination that perfectly fits their views, or those many that never had to transplant from one culture to another, like my pilgrim ancestors, looking for freedom of worship. I am braving this new world, and not all the natives are accepting. They want me to understand their worship of the "sun god," and I am open to learning, but don't feel I should be required to see everything the same in order to be allowed to use my gifts to edify the congregation.

For example, in my experience, people in charismatic churches are very into bringing the kingdom of God to earth. They are obsessed with revival, and are hungry for the move of God. They want to literally take over the earth for the kingdom and restore cities. While I believe in sharing my faith, my hope is in heaven not in this crumbling earth. This is where my Baptist roots show, I suppose, but I just can't get motivated to "bring justice to Seattle." This earth is not my home. Still, I respect the efforts of my friends, and support what they feel called to. I just believe the kingdom of God is in heaven. We have ways to connect with heaven and bring it to earth, but not in a fully complete or literal sense.

There are other nuances like I don't think modern day Christians are all called to drink poison and hold up snakes (Mark 16:18). I think those instructions were for a specific group at a poignant, pivotal time historically. Again, I am happy as a clam with a beaming pearl inside to worship alongside, love on, and do life with my charismatic friends, but are they able to offer me the same acceptance of differences?

As we were trying to get more involved with our new church, we joined a home group and attempted to join the praise team. In both first meetings, I was asked quite directly, "You have been baptized in the Holy Spirit, right?" There could be another book on this topic, but essentially, I was required to have had this experience that aligns with their understanding. I have the Holy Spirit inside me, and have an active relationship with Him. I am able to be moved by the Holy Ghost and regularly am filled with the Spirit. Do I need to speak in tongues to be on the praise team? This was very confusing, and hurtful. The worship leader had made this nonessential a requirement for participation. It's hard to know where I can fit in, belong, and use my gifts in this denominational landscape. I guess I'm too Spirit-filled for the Baptists and not "spiritual" enough for the charismatics!

## INTELLECTUAL AND SPIRIT-FILLED

Discouraged, we decided to visit more churches, which led us to a church near downtown Seattle. Over forty Gen Z youth were jumping and jumping during the worship service, in the open space at the front. I loved that they were able to be on display. I felt an exciting sense of celebration and zeal. Folks were passionate about God and weren't afraid to show it with their whole being. Thank You, Lord. A woman prayed for me after the service, acknowledging God's delight in me when I dance and praying that I would be able to just delight in Him without fear of human judgement.

The pastor had many encouraging words on the subject of manifestations of the Holy Spirit including, "God is more interested in your experience of Him than your explanations." He mentioned the section in Luke 7 where the woman pours out the expensive perfume in extravagant worship and is judged by the Pharisee for it (v. 39). Jesus explains that her acts of sacrificial adoration reveal that she understands that her many sins have been forgiven (v. 47).

I found his sermons to be quite rich, and biblically focused. He even referenced theological writers like R. C. Sproul and A. W. Tozer. A current PhD candidate, clearly he was well read and a scholar of biblical text. I was encouraged by his drive to expand his spiritual knowledge and his ability to present truth eloquently. This is something that I loved about the background I came from, which was full of theological discussions, worldview training, Bible studies, Scripture memory, and the like. I appreciate sermons that are protein-rich and where I can barely keep up with my note-taking.

This mental aspect we had given up, in looking for a church that honored the body and emotions. Often, I found the lyrics of worship songs and content of sermons at the more charismatic churches were not as biblically concentrated or rich in scholarship; an aspect that I personally value. To find a place of balance for mind, spirit, and body was so powerful, rich, encouraging and honestly, how it should be! We are not all just big brains that think about God and mentally ascend to Him any more than we are mindless lalalas. God wants all of us. Let us learn to connect with Him in mind, spirit, and body, bringing before Him the fullness of who He has made us to be.

## NO PRETTY RED BOW

So, there is no perfect ending to my story, no pretty red bow to tie up this section. My journey is not over yet. I am still figuring this out. Currently, my husband and I are visiting churches in the Seattle area. Perhaps, we'll have to start our own church. I envision a space of freedom, where people are free to dance or not, speak in tongues or not; where all gifts are welcome, but not forced. At our gathering, we would honor the Lord through our minds and intellectual depth and also relax and laugh and squeal with joy— letting go and enjoying holy release in His presence. It would be a place of childlike adults, where we can each bring before the Lord all of who He specifically and wonderfully made each of us to be. Mmm. Now, doesn't that sound like heaven?

# PART III

Upward and Onward

# I. REFORMATION

## DOWN WITH THE PEDESTALS

I am done with putting any man on a pedestal. I am finished obeying daddy-pastor or putting my hope in a fallible human being. I resist top-down, man-made structures and control systems that propagate the ego and enslave congregants. The lesson the fractured, blind, imprisoned church teaches us is to look to Jesus! Like the old hymn encourages, "turn your eyes upon Jesus. Look full on His wonderful face, and the things of earth will grow strangely dim in the light of His glory and grace."[1]

We are all pilgrims, journeying on this dried-up planet that seems to be decaying quicker and quicker in 2024, but we serve a living Savior who is full of light and vibrance and abundance and creativity and shining truth. The world will not understand you. The church might not either, but surely God does. He designed you purposefully and thoughtfully and He makes no mistakes. You are amazing, because He made you so! You are wondrous because you're His fantastic handiwork! You are His beloved child. Come home to your good Papa, if you have wandered weary pilgrim.

I have met, along my sojourn, other pilgrims whose candles were not allowed to stand in the church building's lampstand. They were momentarily buried under bushels. They also were misunderstood for carrying "too much" glory. They were not allowed to "give light to all that were in the house" (Matt 5:15).

1 Helen Howarth Lemmel, "Turn Your Eyes upon Jesus," Hymnary.org, https://hymnary.org/text/o_soul_are_you_weary_and_troubled.

Their gifts weren't appreciated or able to be used. Or the church administrative state was worried that the flame would set fire to the place and destroy everything they'd built, so they were on the defensive towards anything new or different.

I have been in a Facebook chat with some of these exiled believers for the past five years, and they are so strong and free and resilient. We pray for each other, and sing songs that we make up, hymns, or reimagined popular sixties songs. We see God in so many things, and have eyes open to His beauty. We find spiritual meaning and parallels that we share to encourage and uplift one another like the church is meant to do.

So, I'm done with rigidity in church culture. I really don't fit tightly-clasped religious ideology, neither did Jesus when He was on the earth. I can't with tradition for tradition's sake, aka: this is just how we do things (unwillingness to rethink) and boxes (even those with pretty steeples). The closed off mindset creates an inability to receive anything new from God, who, by the way, is living and still speaks to those who have ears to hear.

On a side note, I want to clarify this has nothing to do with personal preferences. On that matter, I love liturgical choral and orchestral music, Gregorian monk chants, electric guitars, and light shows. I can praise and worship God to any style of music, because it's about Him not my preferences. I have a degree in classical voice, and actually wish more charismatic worship environments had choirs. It makes me sad how segmented our churches are. I wish we had more freedom and diversity in many more of our American churches.

It's discouraging how many spaces of "love" I have been unwelcomed to because I have different perspectives. Can't we keep the main church things in focus (those being glory to God, worship, community, fellowship, encouragement, and learning), and not be so jot and tittle judgmental as to how one participates in these aspects? Can't we be less controlling of people, and more truly welcoming? Can't we pray more and criticize less?

## I. REFORMATION

Woe to those who, without taking the time to ask for God's leading and hear His voice, ostracize God's special children. Who leave them out in the cold alone because they are hungry for authority, or moved by fear or a spirit of confusion. Who, in laziness and self-interest, do not take the time to hear their valuable stories. Had they listened in the Spirit, they would've learned much and gained wisdom to uplift and enrich their whole community.

Modern American churches, how much more important it is to listen, welcome and love, rather than push people back in line to march toward your ideals. You might think, because of your limited experiences, that these are God's ideals, but surrender your elevated notions. Bow down, literally, on your face and humbly pray. Ask Him what He wants. Ask Him what His tastes and desires are. You will learn something new, and isn't that a good thing!? His ways are not our ways (Isa 55:8).

Friends, let us join with heaven and surrender to God in all things. Let us refuse to submit to this religious spirit. Let us not be bullied by legalism. Let us be angry and refuse to sin, giving our righteous anger up to Jesus. Then thank Him for freedom and revelation while praying for the church. Lord, we ask for pure and tender hearts. We give our cares, and troubles to you. We ask for clean, renewed spirits. Amen.

## LOVE LETTER TO A DECONSTRUCTIONIST

In recent years, more people have begun a process of examining and deconstructing their faith. I have noticed people leaving churches where broken people have hurt them. I get it, and am generally among that crowd. What breaks my heart is seeing those folks abandon God. Some associate their church hurt experience with God Himself, like they are toxically intertwined.

I get it if you can't find a church, or the trauma makes you feel like you could never go back or try again. I get how you can feel more depressed after a church service than before you went in. I get how damaging it can be to be harmed in a space that God intended to be for healing. I understand questioning the point of it all.

What I want you to know is that the Father isn't pleased with the way you were treated. His heart grieves for your squelched spirit. He is righteously angry at the pride and fear that pushed you down. Those actions were not aligned with the law of love and light. He is not okay with what church "leaders" did to you, and I am sorry for what you experienced.

God designed the church to be a refuge for weary souls. We, Christians, get beat up enough in the world. When we come into a church, it's meant to be a safe harbor, a lighthouse from the storms of life. It isn't easy being a human, nor is it easy being different, aliens on this planet. Nor is the narrow path, which leads to life, a walk in the park (Matt 7:13–14).

My fellow rejected friends, I need you to know that God is real and powerful and He adores *you*. If you leave the church, fine, but don't throw out the joyful, precious baby with the nasty water. He will heal you. He wants to bind up your wounds (Ps 147:3). He is on your side. He is close to the broken hearted. I encourage you to read Psalms, my favorite book of the Bible. David, a man after God's own heart, expresses agony, frustration, passion, and elation. His emotion and human experience is so freely, and beautifully expressed. I am grateful for this biblical wild child.

Please don't blame God for what man does. He gives human beings freedom, which explains why there is wickedness and pain on this earth. He does not cause the evil acts, but He is there for us in our suffering. "He is our refuge and strength, a very present help in trouble" (Ps 46:1). He wants people who choose him, not who are forced to love Him. Because we are not robots, we have the ability to hurt each other, ourselves, and God.

He wants to be there for us. He wants to take care of us—His sweet children—like a good, good shepherd or a fluffy mother hen. I hope and pray you can learn to trust Him again, or for the first time. Under His wings, you will find refuge (Ps 91). He is the shelter for your church-weary soul.

## I. REFORMATION

## CONNECT AND FOLLOW

Worship can be reduced to this simple concept: connect with Jesus and follow Him. Connect and follow. Worship includes obedience. Not to a pastor or to the suppressive walls of a church building, but to the King of the universe, God Himself. Let us keep our eyes on Him, and follow as He leads.

When Jesus was on the earth, He wasn't looking to the right and to the left nervous about who might be distracted or uncomfortable. He didn't stop living out His calling because humans were uncomfortable. He actually did many things that were out of peoples' comfort zones. He stretched their faith, and for those who had eyes to see, their concept of God. He didn't follow every rule. He healed on the Sabbath. He spoke with gentiles and women with bad reputations. He was focused on the heart, not caught up in the minutia of things that didn't matter—while trampling on valuable humans. He listened, empathized, and truly cared.

He thought outside the box, and didn't require individuals to squeeze into too-tight parameters. He made space for children, and people with disabilities. He didn't often choose the most fit and ideal in man's eyes. He surprised with His choices. He delighted and shocked. He brought heaven to earth, and many weren't ready for it.

They didn't recognize heaven when it was right in front of them. So, they rejected who they claimed to worship. They didn't allow God into their synagogues. They wanted Him dead. They wanted to kill the living God in the name of order, protocol, and decency.


## . *HEAVEN*

Let us look ahead to heaven, our eternal home, as an example! Up there, all Christians will be worshiping together in the diversity and unity God intended. Let us start the praise party now, "for he raised us from the dead along with Christ and seated us with him in the Heavenly realms because we are united with Christ Jesus" (Eph 2:6 NLT). This is our reality. This is our destiny. This identity is who we truly are. Let's step into the GLORY, friends. With or without a church who is ready to elevate, we have the ability to commune with Christ and bring Him all the praise and honor He is so worthy of. What is the essence of heaven but that boundless and pure, eternally irrepressible flow?

# II. The Triune Dance

## VISION

In 2016, I had a long commute from Fort Lauderdale to Miami. During these drives along the wetland swamps of the Everglades, with mossy bald cypress trees and floating gators, the vision of the triangle and circle rested on my forehead. Much like the title, *Big God, Big Glory*, this visual stayed with me. I now have a tattoo of this image and feel it's connected to the life message I'm meant to carry about freedom, glory, belonging, and the value of the body.

## TRIANGLE

The triangle represents, firstly, the Trinity—the equal, loving relationship between Father, Son, and Holy Spirit. Each person of the Godhead is distinct, and yet all three so beautifully harmonize. Diversity in unity is God's heart. I love that equality isn't sameness. I love that we can be ourselves and be celebrated and accepted for who we truly are in Him. God loves and accepts Himself, and created us in His image—creative, powerful, and unique!

A triangle rests on a stable foundation and points upward. We are powerful and at peace when our eyes are looking heavenward, acknowledging Him from whom we come and to whom we are headed. When we steady ourselves in God's love, we are stable, powerful, and fully energetic. If the triangle is upside down, however, we are pointed in the wrong direction and the base is not trustworthy. We feel insecure and anxious; and are prone to toppling over. The shape of the triangle is a reminder to stay firmly planted, balanced and rooted in Him.

Triangles are also used as directional and navigational tools. Think arrow. Think compass. Think aim. I will fix my eyes on Jesus the author and finisher of my faith and the origin of my truest joy and deepest bliss (Heb 12:2).

## CIRCLE

If the Triangle is largely representative of the Trinity, then the circle is the divine dance that God flows in. The circle is heaven's movement. Let's circle back to "Perichoresis," the Greek word introduced earlier in this book that was historically used to describe the trinity. It is derived from the Greek *peri*, meaning "around" and *chorein*, which has multiple meanings. Among them are "to make room for," "go forward," and "contain."

We contain the glory of God in our bodies. Let us make room for His expression. We are a revelation of Him—a display of His character and beauty. We are called to "go forward" on this earth for hope and freedom. All the while, He is going out before us, making a way in the wilderness (Isa 43:19). We are encircled by His love, surrounded by His presence. We can move boldly, knowing that we are accepted and contained in Him.

The circle also represents wholeness, original perfection, and the actualization of authentic self. This is the process of transformation into His image, of blossoming into all He created us to *be*. As we learn to trust God and release the fear of others' possible negative reactions to our expressions, we release joy and creativity on this earth. As we grow in our God-given identities, we bring pleasure to God and lasting fulfillment to ourselves as we journey on this earth. We can trust that God will fulfill His purpose in us (Ps 138:8). He is sovereign over our sanctification process.

More personally, the circle reveals to me something yet to be completed. I'm on a journey toward wholeness. The circles's ends will finally be united when, sanctified, I enter heaven. While the triangle is indicative of eternal vision, direction, and spirit of pursuit, the circle is my eternal connection to heaven that softens and balances out my edges while I move on this earth.

## DANCE NOT DICTATORSHIP

The dance of the Trinity also reinforces the concept that God operates not in top-down hierarchy, but in mutually respectful relationship. Each person is different, yet unified in love. As the three persons of the Godhead function, so the church is meant to be a community where each member can be appreciated for who they uniquely are—each with a distinctive purpose. Unlike the one-man-rule systems prevalent today, the church is meant to honor each individual, providing opportunities for all to participate.

I believe American Christian culture's misunderstandings about how church should be is in direct relation to misunderstandings about God. We have already addressed the shiny attributes of God that are neglected in our church teachings. Zooming out one can see that, in addition to our church structure, European American society as a whole is functioning from a wrongness in terms of viewing God.

It was good that early American settlers escaped the oppressive Catholic rule of the church of England. It was good that they bravely risked it all to come to a new land where they could experience freedom of worship. They were pursuing liberty, attempting to be free from intensely religious formations. Though the physical journey to new soil is complete, the heart/mind/body journey is not. In a multiplicity of ways, the American church still carries the trappings of European church legalism and view of a dominating God who is more ruler than lover. For example, we do not, in our bones, know God to be gentle. Nor do we, generally, see Him as joyful.

My ancestors were Puritans. Their hearts were in the right place, but they had a lot to learn. We still have so much to shake off from our rigid past. They founded this country and only did the best they could with what they knew. They were products of their environment. They came far in their lifetimes, but we in the church cannot let the growth end where they did. Let us keep pushing out of the bud. We must continue, transform, blossom into our truest form—so we can fully operate in our freedoms and be as God designed us. How can our churches look more like heaven, the garden of Eden, the Trinity? With such questions you could breathe, pray, and listen.

## EMBRACING GRACE

Our Christian cultural ideas are limited in perspective and based on human-centric church traditions. One way we can move to get the whips, shame, and corruption of our harsh heritage out of our bodies is to quit hustling to prove our worth and trying to earn God's approval. We need to accept that He is our beloved sacrificial Lamb and we are His beloved babies.

I invite you to just stop. Breathe. Focus on that humbling and invigorating picture. Our precious King became weak and vulnerable and gave up His very life allowing Himself to be murdered on our behalf. Can you feel His spotless wool? It is so warm and comforting to press your face into.

He died to end shame, not to make us feel guilty all the time at the contrast of His perfection and our sin. We are not our sin. If you have accepted Jesus Christ's work on the cross to pay for your sins, if you are trusting in His work alone for your eternal salvation, you are now the righteousness of God. Wow! Soak in the gift of His eternal goodness, friend. You need only receive His love! I know, that's a difficult truth to embrace coming from our old-world Catholic roots. He doesn't demand your suffering in order to be loved by Him. Praise to King Jesus! He made the sacrifice on your behalf. He led with strength and mercy, that we might respond to Him. We are the feminine energy here, His bride. My goodness, He loves us and oh, how we celebrate You, our sweet, sweet Savior.

## II. The Triune Dance

*Dear Lord, help us surrender to Your divine flow. We repent of thinking we know better. We want Your wonder and mystery. Help us to allow and desire for You to blow our minds. We release the pride of our tiny, human minds. Take us into the heavenlies with You. All we want is to rest under your motherly wings, Holy Spirit.*

To the Trinity, I ask that you help us release the fear of people's opinions. We want to surrender more and more to Your leading. We say yes with our spirit to Your invitation to dance with you. We join that holy circle, as You take our hands again and forever.

I love you. I love you. I love you.

# III. SHINE ON

An idealistic individual, I often daydream about the peaceful, perfect garden of Eden, the future (restored) new earth or my home in heaven. I long to be in a place where I can witness and partake of the fullness of glory without constraint, fear, hiding, or judgement. In heaven, all of our days will be spent in His light, as He delights in us and we give Him all praise.

Will you join me in asking God: How can we bring heaven to earth? How can we be faithful in our hearts and bodies? How can we more fully manifest your glory on this dark planet? We ask, Lord, that you help us to submit to You in our bodily vessels. Please remove our pride and desire to control, so we can shine more brightly; attracting others to Your light. Thank You for making us special. Thank You for the burden and honor of bearing Your image. We thank You for the ability to faithfully share in your sufferings and glory (Rom 8:17). Please help us as we carry Your light.

> *Glory to God in the highest heaven, and on earth*
> *peace to those on whom His favor rests.*
> (Luke 2:14 NIV)

## BLESSING

I hope through this book you've come to know God more deeply, and that you are further transformed into His image. I hope that your mind has been stretched and your stride lengthened, so that you may move with brighter power in the kingdom of our King. I hope you continue to allow God to renew your heart, and that my words were used to smooth it—like one of David's mighty stones. I pray that you will be strong and effective and bold, as you move powerfully and purposefully from the sling, with a tender heart and a brave spirit. I pray a special blessing over you warriors as you serve God in your bodies; that He will protect you and that you'll always take refuge under His wings. His banner over you is love (Song 2:4) and you'll experience sweet victory through Jesus. "He will cover you with His feathers. He will shelter you with His wings. His faithful promises are your armor and protection" (Ps 91:4 NLT).

Speaking of wings, remember the living creatures in Rev 4 who are "full of eyes all around and within" (v. 8)? They keep seeing God from new perspectives, soaking endlessly in the aspects of His divine revealing. Day and night, night and day, they never run out of fresh experiences with the great I AM. Let us be like these adoring creatures. Joining in their eternal awe, let us give Him our faces in attention, our hearts in desire, our minds in curiosity, and our bodies in passion. Let us be a kingdom of children in endless wonder, never ceasing to respond in praise, "Holy, holy, holy is the Lord God Almighty, who was and is and is to come" (v. 8). To God be all glory, of every form, expression, variety, and flavor, forever and ever. Amen.

# About the Author

KENDALL IS A DANCER, published poet, and educator with over twenty years of professional teaching experience. She received an MFA in creative writing from the University of Tampa and a BS in music performance, with a minor in biblical studies. Kendall teaches writing online for Florida International University and on campus at Seattle Pacific University.

Traditional boxed-in Baptist turned dancing, glory enthusiast, and anti-shame warrior, Kendall desires to see people moving in freedom, unabashed joy, and creative expression. She dances and speaks at events, leads workshops, and creates informative videos.

She has served as a worship leader for both traditional and contemporary services. Kendall also has a variety of experience in praise and worship environments: directing church choirs, cantoring at a Catholic church, playing her viola and singing in praise bands, leading a retirement home ministry, conducting the strings program at a Christian music camp, providing classical solos for a Presbyterian church, and leading worship on the piano at Celebrate Recovery.

Kendall lives in the Pacific Northwest with her husband Michael and their two precious Persian cats, Tabby and Red. In her free time, she can be found delighting in her backyard garden, writing poetry, or in wild nature communing with God and animals.

# Acknowledgements

I AM GRATEFUL FOR the generous editing assistance and kind reviews from Kathleen M. and Karyn S. I also give unending thanks to my sweet husband, Michael, for his constant encouragement and support with this project.